D1436540

# HYMNS OF THE
## TEMPLE

# HYMNS OF THE TEMPLE

*by*

NORMAN SNAITH, D.D.

SCM PRESS LTD
56 BLOOMSBURY STREET, LONDON WC1

*First published July 1951*

*Printed in Great Britain by*
*Northumberland Press Limited*
*Gateshead on Tyne*

# CONTENTS

# PREFACE

IT HAS BEEN SAID that the Psalter in its present form was the hymn book of the Second Temple. Whether every psalm was written definitely for use in public worship is a question which may never be settled, because our own experience tells us that often the more personal the hymn is, the greater the favourite it is with the congregation. No hymn could be more intimate and personal than 'Jesu, Lover of my soul' or 'Abide with me', and yet there are few hymns which are sung more often, or are more widely known. Of all the HYMNS OF THE TEMPLE, none are more certainly so than the Psalms of Asaph (50; 73-83). There was a tradition that David instituted the Temple choirs when first he brought the Ark up to Zion's hill (I Chron. 16.4-42), and that he installed 'Asaph and his brethren' to constitute the Temple choir. Of this we may be sure, that in the time of the Chronicler (? 350 B.C.), Asaph and his brethren were the choristers, because we know that the Chronicler did largely clothe the events of other days with the garments of his own time.

This volume contains studies of some of these Asaphite psalms, and, together with them, of some Qorachite psalms. (The usual spelling in our English Versions is 'Korah'.) These Qorachites seem, at one time, to have been officiating priests, but in the days of the second Temple they were reckoned with the Levites, and performed various temple duties, especially those of door-keepers. But evidently at one time they were singers in the Temple choirs.

The first chapter is a general introduction to the Psalter as a whole. It deals with such general questions as the place which the Psalter occupies in the Bible, the way in which

it was compiled, the poetry of the psalms, and it concludes
with short summaries of the modern study of the Psalter.
The section on the poetry of the psalms shows how closely
the style of the poetry is connected with the recently discovered Canaanite poems from Ugarit, a hundred and fifty
miles north of ancient Tyre.

Succeeding chapters deal with particular psalms, four (or,
more accurately, three) of them Qorachite (42-43, 44, 46) and
two of them Asaphite (50, 73). In each case, interest is
focused on such topics as may be judged to help in understanding the aim of the psalmist, and his teaching for his
own time and for our time. Often various archaic phrases
are used by the psalmists, going away back into early mythology and folklore. Sometimes the psalms can be understood
better because of archaeological evidence which has come to
light in recent years in Palestine and elsewhere. The ideas
involved are discussed, not only in relation to the psalm
itself, but with reference to other passages in the Bible and
their Christian development. There are occasional translations given of particular verses. These are original. They
claim no particular merit, perhaps, from the literary point
of view, but they are designed to give the reader an idea of
the native rhythm and style of these age-old Israelite songs.
There are cases where a precise knowledge of the actual
Hebrew word used is of immense assistance in the understanding of the message of the psalmist. These discussions
are non-academic, and by transliteration and so forth, every
effort has been taken to ensure that they are readily intel-
ligible to those who do not read Hebrew.

Reference is made on page 60 to the J-tradition. This is
the southern tradition of the beginnings of Hebrew history,
dating away back to the first days, but crystallized into
writing in the south *c*. 850 B.C. The letter J is used because
the Sacred Name Jehovah (Jahweh) is used throughout.
Parallel with this is the northern tradition, usually referred
to as the E-tradition, because the word *Elohim* is normally
used for God, this being the ordinary Hebrew word for

' gods ', used in the plural to denote majesty. This tradition was crystallized into writing *c.* 750 B.C. At some time during the next century these two traditions were combined, perhaps during Hezekiah's time, which we know to have been a time of considerable literary activity (Prov. 25.1). Later this JE-tradition was combined with the Deuteronomic writings (*c.* 550 B.C.), and still later, after the exile, the Priestly writers combined the whole into what is now substantially the Pentateuch (Genesis-Deuteronomy), adding their own material, the P-tradition. Some scholars trace these traditions through succeeding books as far as I Kings, but there is no general unanimity concerning the soundness of this procedure. In recent years, scholars have been suggesting more and more that the origin of most of these traditions is to be found in the stories the priests told at the various shrines, and there is every likelihood that this is actually how these traditions were preserved and handed on.

The book, especially from chapter II onwards, is designed to give a sort of running commentary on the psalms, branching out into whatever avenue is most likely to interest and help the reader. There is very ancient warrant for this, since the ancient Jewish Commentary on the Psalms (*Midrash Tehillin*) is of this type. The reader will find it advisable and helpful to have his copy of the Psalter open beside him, and he will also want to hunt up the various passages of Scripture to which his attention is from time to time directed. The book is written in the hope that, for some at any rate, the Psalter will be able to speak forth the Word of the Living God with a new clarity.

*Leeds* NORMAN SNAITH

### Acknowledgment

We wish to record our thanks to Messrs. Methuen & Co. Ltd. and to the author, for permission to quote a verse from *When we were very young* by Mr. A. A. Milne.

# I

## THE PSALTER

### (a) *Its place in the Bible*

THE PLACE of Psalms in the English Bible is determined primarily by the fact that for the first four hundred years of the Christian Church the Bible was the Greek Bible (the Septuagint). Following that, for another thousand years the Christian Bible was the Latin Bible, the Vulgate, Jerome's translation from the Hebrew, except for the Psalter itself which is from the Greek. Jerome made three translations of the Bible in all, two from the Greek and the third from the Hebrew. The Vulgate Psalter is from his second Greek translation. The new translation from the Hebrew was never able to oust the earlier Greek-based rendering, just as in the Established Church the Authorized Version of the Psalms was never able to take the place of the earlier version, the Prayer Book Version, as we call it to-day. The reason is probably the same in each case. The earlier version was established in the liturgies, and liturgies are characteristically conservative. Men do not easily change forms of rites and words which have endeared themselves by regular usage.

The Vulgate, in a revised form, is still the Bible of the Roman Church, and the authoritative English Version amongst Romanists is the Douay Version. This is a translation of the Latin Vulgate, and makes no pretence of being a translation from the original languages, Hebrew and Greek. The Protestant Churches, on the other hand, have

turned back to the original tongues for their translations, to
the original Hebrew so far as the Old Testament is concerned, and to the original Greek for the New Testament.
But even though the Protestants have turned to the Hebrew
Scriptures for the Old Testament, they have nevertheless
followed Jerome's order for the various books of the Old
Testament which they hold to be sacred and authoritative.
Jerome's order is the Greek order. The Protestant Churches
followed the Palestinian Jewish tradition which accepted
only the Hebrew Scriptures, and they rejected those Greek-
written books which were accepted in Alexandria as being
sacred and authoritative. These books, as is well known,
are to be found in the Apocrypha. The Roman Church
continues to accept these writings as authoritative equally
with the rest, whilst the Anglican Church accepts them to
be read 'for example of life and instruction of manners'
(Sixth Article), but not for doctrine.

The Septuagint translators, or their successors, sought to
put all the books of their Bible (Old Testament and
Apocrypha) into what they believed to be the correct historical order, with the historical books all coming first. This
is the first beginning of Biblical Criticism, apart from the
notes at the head of some of the psalms which associate them
with particular events in the life of David. Further, whenever the title of the Hebrew book was obscure or had no
meaning for Greek readers, the translators substituted a
Greek title which did mean something for the ordinary
reader, usually a title which described the contents of the
book. Thus, the Hebrew title for the second book in the
Bible is *we'eleh shemoth,* the first two words of the book,
meaning 'and these are the names of'. These Hebrew
words meant as little to the Greek reader as they do to an
English reader, so we call the book Exodus, which is
Jerome's latinization of the Greek title 'exit, going out'.
Similarly, instead of *'eykhah* ('how'), we have Lamentations, from Jerome's *lamentationes,* his translation of the
Greek *threnoi*. And so also, our Psalms is the anglicized

form of Jerome's *psalmi*, itself a latinized form of the Greek *psalmoi*, which is the Septuagint translation of the plural of the Hebrew *mizmor*. This is not the Hebrew title, which is *tehillim* ('praises'), but it is the one which is found at the head of fifty-seven of the psalms.

In our English Versions, Psalms follows Job owing to the Septuagint judgment that Job, with its patriarchal setting, ought to precede David's psalms. This is the Septuagint-Vulgate order. The Greeks, as we have said, placed all the historical books first, placing Ruth next after Judges and Ezra-Nehemiah after I and II Chronicles. For the rest, they started with Job and finished with Malachi, doing their best to keep to the historical order, but keeping the three major prophets together, Isaiah, Jeremiah and Ezekiel, though they inserted Lamentations next after Jeremiah in the belief that he was the author of these five laments.

The order in the Hebrew Bibles is very different. The Hebrew Bible is in three main divisions, each separated from the other as clearly and as definitely as the New Testament is separated from the Old Testament in our English Bibles. These three divisions, the Law and the Prophets and the Writings (this is the actual title of the Hebrew Bible to this day), represent the three successive stages in the growth of the Hebrew Bible. The last group to be recognized as sacred and authoritative was the Writings. This does not necessarily mean that the books which are to be found in this last group were the last to be written, though some of the latest books (e.g. Daniel) are actually to be found here. It means simply that the group as a whole, and therefore the individual books to be found in it, was the last to be recognized officially. In all printed editions of the Hebrew Bible, Psalms is the first book in this last section. Actually there are three Jewish traditions as to the order of the books in the Writings; namely, Hebrew-printed Bibles which follow the Ashkenazi (Franco-German) tradition (probably because the first printed Bibles were from Ashkenazi manuscripts) with Psalms first; the

Talmud tradition, which has Ruth first and Psalms second; the Sephardi (Spanish) tradition, which has Chronicles first and Psalms second.

## (b) *The compilation of the Psalter*

Two methods have been employed in the compilation of the Psalter, one for the first three books (Psalms 1-89), and the other for the last two books (Psalms 90-150). The method for Books I-III was the embodiment as a whole of earlier psalters, making one out of a number of others; and for Books IV-V, mainly the addition of liturgical groups.

First, then, the compilation of Books I-III (Psalms 1-89). There were five earlier psalters, two of them 'David's', two of them levitical ('Asaph's' and 'The Sons of Qorach's'), and 'The Music-master's'. The first psalter was the Jehovist Davidic Psalter. It contained all the forty-one psalms in Book I, except for Psalms 1 and 33 which were inserted later. This psalter is called 'Jehovist' because of its regular use of the Divine Name Jehovah. (The true pronunciation of the Tetragrammaton JHVH is uncertain, and is still discussed. The recently published, 1948, fifth volume of *Oudtestamentische Studiën*, the publication of the Netherlands Society for Old Testament Study, opens with three articles, all three of which advocate different spellings, Jahu, Yahwe and Jehova. I have used the traditional English spelling, because it has at least a religious tradition behind it.) This Davidic psalter was probably the original official psalter. Each psalm (the title of the second having been transferred to the 'head of the corner') has as its head 'David's'. The Book ends with a benediction (41.13), which may well have been used, though at a later period, at the conclusion of each psalm, and is probably the ultimate origin of the present-day custom of concluding with the *Gloria*.

The next stage in the evolution of the Psalter was the addition of psalms 42-83. This is an Elohist psalter, i.e.

the word *Elohim* (ordinary word for 'God') has been generally, though not universally, substituted for the Sacred Name
JHVH. It is probable that in some of the cases where the
name JHVH is actually found, we have a later interpolation.
The evidence for some substitutions is to be seen in 43.4
(Elohim, my God), 80.7 (this is quite clear in the Hebrew,
where the original must have been 'JHVH of Hosts'), and
similarly 80.14. There are two instances where a psalm,
or part of a psalm, is found in both Davidic psalters; 53,
which is mostly 14; and 70, which is part of 40. The deliberate substitution of *Elohim* for JHVH can be seen in these
psalms, though in 70.1 the JHVH has survived. This Elohist
psalter was itself a compilation of three earlier psalters, a
Davidic psalter (51-72), and the two levitical psalters, 'The
Sons of Qorach's' (42-49) and 'Asaph's' (50 and 73-83).
In the year 1866, Heinrich Ewald suggested that 51-72
originally preceded 42. This is a brilliant suggestion, and it
has been generally accepted. It, so to speak, kills two birds
with one stone. It brings all the Davidic psalms together
(1-41 and 52-72), thus making the note at the end of 72
exactly true, so far as the first three books of the Psalter are
concerned: 'The prayers of David the son of Jesse are
ended.' Further, it joins the 'lonely' Asaphite psalm to
its fellows, making the order 50, 73-83.

The second official psalter was thus formed out of four
earlier psalters, two Davidic and two levitical. But there was
also a fifth collection, 'The Music-master's'. Whenever
any psalm found in the four collections was also found in
this fifth collection, a note to that effect was inserted at the
beginning of the psalm. Sometimes also the tune, prescribed in 'The Music-master's', was also specified: e.g.
'Destroy not' (57, 58, 59, 75), evidently a vintage tune,
Isaiah 65.8; 'Dove of the distant terebinths' (56); 'Maids
for the son' (9); 'Hinds of the dawn' (22); 'Lilies' (45, 69),
'Lily, witness' (60), 'Lilies, witness' (80). Perhaps these
last three titles all refer to the same air, unless perchance,
there are two tunes involved, 'Lilies' and 'Witness'. Notes

of this type are not found elsewhere, so we are justified in saying that they belonged originally to the collection of psalms which is described as 'The Music-master's'. There is nothing more natural than for this collection to have this particular type of note. From this source, there are other instructions, which apparently refer to the orchestra: 'strings' (4, 6, 54, 55, 61, 67, 76), 'flutes' (5), together with others, the meanings of which are uncertain. We know from later times that specific details were laid down as to the nature of the accompaniment proper for certain occasions. We know, for instance, that flutes were used in Herod's Temple on ten occasions: the day of killing the first Passover, the day of killing the second Passover, the first day of the Feast of Unleavened Bread, the Feast of Pentecost, and the eight days of the Feast of Tabernacles, but not the Sabbath and not the first day of the feast.

The second method of compilation begins with Book IV at psalm 90. The first liturgical group is 90-100. It contains what have been held to be the ten original Sabbath psalms (90-99) and the traditional psalm for an ordinary day of the week (100), i.e. 'ordinary' in the sense that it is not a special day of any kind, not a Sabbath, nor a festival, nor anything else. This last is the present-day tradition, and there is every reason to suppose that the custom is very ancient. Of the ten psalms 90-99, only one (94) is not now definitely a Sabbath psalm, and its place is taken by 29. Proceeding, 103 and 104 are Blessing psalms; 105 and 106 are Hallelujah psalms, where the *hallelu-jah* (praise ye Jah) should be at the beginning of each psalm and not at the end of the previous psalm, cf. the Septuagint, which here has preserved the ancient placing. Psalm 107 contains variations on the theme

> Give–ye–thanks to–JHVH, for–he–is–good,
> For his–covenant–mercy (*chesed*) is–for–ever.

This couplet seems to have been the ritual call to sing

psalms in the time of the Chronicler (I Chron. 16.41; II Chron. 5.13; 7.3; 7.6; 20.21; Ezra 3.11), comparable to the verse

> O Lord, open thou my lips,
> And my mouth shall declare thy praise,

which prefaces the Amidah, the central core of the synagogue service, and which ocupies a somewhat similar place in the liturgy of Morning Prayer according to the rite of the Established Church.

Psalms 108-110 are a little Davidic group; 111-118 (?115) is another Hallelujah group; whilst 119 is the great eight-line acrostic based on the Deuteronomic law. The next group (120-134) is commonly called 'The Pilgrim Psalter' on the assumption that these fifteen psalms were sung by pilgrims as they travelled in companies (cf. Luke 2.44, for the return journey) up to the Feasts at Jerusalem. According to the Mishnah[1] tract *Sukkah*, during the all-night illuminations of the festival of the first night of the Feast of the Tabernacles, the levitical choirs of the Second Temple stood on the fifteen steps which led up from the Court of the Women through the Gate of Nicanor into the Court of the Israelites, and there they sang psalms 'corresponding to the fifteen Songs of Degrees in the Psalms'. This statement is not wholly clear whether they sang these particular fifteen psalms, one psalm according to each step, but it is so stated in the Mishnah tract *Middoth*. This is probably the origin of the titles of these psalms; they are 'steps' songs. 135-136 form a pair of Hallelujah psalms; 137-145 are Davidic psalms (see Septuagint for 137), and the Psalter concludes with the five great Hallelujah psalms, known as the Hallel and sung at festivals.

The Septuagint has one hundred and fifty psalms, but the last one is explicitly said to be 'outside the number', and it is a composite psalm, mostly composed of elements from various other psalms. The numeration of the psalms in the

---

[1] Sayings and discussions of the Rabbis from *c*. 100 B.C. to *c*. 200 A.D.

Septuagint is, for the most part, different from that in the Hebrew text. 9 and 10 are written there as one psalm, which they originally were, 114 and 115 are written as one, but both 116 and 117 are split into two, and so the proper number is regained.

The Psalter is divided into five books, cf. the Revised Version, which in this respect is true to both the Hebrew and the Greek traditions. According to the *Midrash on the Psalms*,[2] 'Moses gave the Israelites the five books of the Law, and to correspond to these David gave them the Book of the Psalms in five books.' I have argued elsewhere that this correspondence is much more real and close than is generally recognized. It has been suspected for many years that just as the Law (i.e. the Pentateuch) was read one portion every Sabbath in Palestine following a three-year lectionary, together with a suitable 'closing' (*Haftarah*) reading from the Prophets, so also the psalms may have been recited one psalm every Sabbath during the three years. There is an ancient tradition that out of eight portions of the Law ten Sabbath lessons were formed. This is a very strange statement, but it seems to mean that eight portions were allocated to each two-month period, and that where there were more than eight Sabbaths in a two-month period, the portions were rearranged within the eight. It is true that there never could be ten Sabbaths in a two-month period, but this kind of over-exactitude is typical of ancient Jewish meticulousness. We can therefore work out the portions and the psalms, four each to a month, and let the variations look after themselves. Working on this basis, we find the curious state of affairs that Exodus was begun on the 42nd Sabbath, Leviticus on the 73rd, Numbers on the 90th, and Deuteronomy on the 117th. But 1, 42, 73, 90, 107, are the first psalms in the five Books of the Psalms. This can scarcely be a coincidence. Four of the numbers coincide. The great Deuteronomic psalm is undoubtedly the 119th. If this was recited of olden time on the 117th Sabbath, then the three-

[2] The ancient Jewish commentary on the Psalms.

year cycle was concluded with 146, which leaves four psalms for the intercalary month which was due every third year. These four Sabbaths are probably the origin of the present four Special Sabbaths of the present-day Jewish ecclesiastical calendar. The difference between three solar years and three four-week-month years is exactly this period. There is a certain amount of evidence which suggests that at the time of the Chronicler the official Psalter ended at 106, so this would account for the break there, especially if this marked the end of the Psalter for any period of time. Compare the end of 106 with I Chronicles 16.36, which shows the way in which psalms were evidently concluded in the time of the Chronicler.

Out of this suggestion of the triennial lectionary for the Psalter, two items in particular emerge which are worthy of note. One is that Psalm 1 is the psalm which was inserted when the Psalter was arranged for this purpose. The psalm is actually concerned with the desirability of regular study of the Law, and forms a fitting prelude to the study of the Law itself. No psalm is more suitable to be recited on the Sabbath when the first portion of the Law was read. The other item of interest is that 23 coincides with the story of Bethel (Gen. 28.8-22). The psalm originally had, of course, nothing to do with Jacob, but if the scribes were searching for a psalm which could be so placed in the Psalter as to coincide with the story of Jacob at Bethel, this psalm is beyond doubt the most apt of any extant psalms. Most of the verses of the psalm contain admirable sentiments for a young man setting off into the unknown, and there is enough of the desert and the pasture-country to make it fit approximately into the experience of one whose property would be mostly sheep and goats. Perhaps also the curious last verse can be explained along these lines. The Hebrew reads: 'And I will return in the house of JHVH (*beth-JHVH*) . . .' The verse is always translated 'And I will dwell . . .', but this definitely is not what the Hebrew says. To say, as some do, 'And I will return to dwell' may make good sense, but it is taking an unjustifiable liberty with the Hebrew. What seems to have happened is that one letter (*yodh*, the smallest of them all) has dropped out, so that ' And I will dwell ' has become ' And I will return '. Our suggestion is that this omission is actually due to the influence of the Hebrew in Gen. 28.21 ' so that I return . . . God's house (Beth El) '.

## (c) *The poetry of the psalms*

The literary style of the psalms has a long history, and it reaches back into the culture which was common to all the Near East from Mesopotamia through to Egypt. In particular, it has strong affinities with the poems which have been found during the last twenty years at Ras-Shamra, the site of the ancient city of Ugarit.[3] The city of Ugarit was an important sea-port in the time of Hammurabi (*c.* 1650 B.C.), and was the gateway for the trade between Mesopotamia and the Mediterranean. When the early Assyrian war-lords marched west, it was not simply to obtain the hard cedar-wood from the Lebanon, but to open up the trade routes to the sea and beyond. The normal caravan route followed the curve of the Fertile Crescent, leaving the Euphrates and the recently excavated Mari, and thence straight west through Palmyra and Damascus. Ugarit is almost due west of Damascus, and the traveller needed only to keep on due west from Mari to arrive at Ugarit. If he wanted to go down to Egypt, he turned southwest after Damascus, and so down through Palestine. Ugarit was at its heyday in the fifteenth and fourteenth centuries, the Tell-el-Amarna age, and declined with the passing of the bronze age, being overwhelmed and finally destroyed about the end of the thirteenth century. These texts therefore give us a picture of city life in North Syria

[3] For a comprehensive English translation of these texts, see Cyrus H. Gordon, *Ugaritic Literature*, published in 1949 by the Pontificium Institutum Biblicum.

not long before Joshua and his Ephraimites invaded South Syria across Jordan. Fortunately, most of the texts are religious texts, and have to do both with ritual and myths.

The most recent study of the forms of Hebrew poetry is by T. H. Robinson.[4] He lays down as the fundamental principle: 'Every verse must consist of at least two "members", the second of which must, more or less completely, satisfy the expectation raised by the first.' Sometimes the sense runs on directly as in the poetry of any other language, but more often there is a definite and deliberate parallelism in the couplet, whereby the statement of the first line is repeated exactly, but with other words in the second line. This type of parallelism is called 'synonymous'. For instance:

> The–boar from–the–wood ravages–it,
> And–the–creatures of–the–wild feed–on–it. (80.13).

Here the parallelism is complete and exact, and it goes hand in hand with the metre which is 3:3 and 3:3. (The words tied with hyphens represent one word and one stress in the Hebrew.) In many cases the parallelism is not complete, sometimes with a member missing in the second line, and sometimes with one member missing and another element introduced to fill out the picture which the psalmist is painting. This type is very common, and is called 'climbing' or 'constructive' parallelism. An example of the first type, where one member is omitted, is

> I–will–not–take from–thy–house a–bullock,
> From–thy–folds he-goats:
> For–mine (is) every–beast–of the–bad–lands,
> The–cattle on–a–thousand–hills. (50.9-10).

An example of the second is:

> In–thee trusted our–fathers,
> They–trusted and–thou–deliverest–them. (22.4).

---

[4] *Poetry and the Poets of the Old Testament,* 1947, especially pp. 11-46.

Somewhat similar is:

> My–mouth shall–be–filled with–thy–praise,
> All–the–day with–thy–beauty. (71.8).

Or the parallelism may be partly 'climbing' and wholly
'antithetic':

> For–JHVH knoweth the–way–of the–righteous,
> But–the–way–of the–wicked shall–perish. (1.6).

where incidentally, *derekh* (way) means a track across the
desert, a caravan route, cf. Ex. 13.17, where the two routes
from Egypt are mentioned, the regular caravan routes:
The Way of the Land of the Philistines along the sea
coast, and The Way of the Red Sea Desert. An excellent
example of climbing, antithetical parallelism is:

> JHVH supports the–humble,
> Abases the–wicked to–the–ground. (147.6).

The same type of literary structure can be seen in a
Coronation Ode of the time of Rameses IV (XX dynasty,
1168 b.c.):

> They that had fled have returned to their towns,
> And they that were hidden have come forth once more.
> They that were hungry are sated and happy,
> They that were thirsty are drunken.
> They that were naked are clad in fine linen,
> And they that were ragged have fine garments.

or in this hymn to Thoth, the god of wisdom:

> It (i.e. the well of wisdom) is closed for him that hath
>     words to say;
> It is open for the silent.
> The silent comes and finds the well;
> The hot-head comes, but thou art choked.

Similarly in Mesopotamia, we have the same literary style. For example, here is part of Asshur-bani-pal's Coronation Ode (he reigned from 668 to 622 B.C.):

> Adad let loose his showers,
> Ea opened his fountains:
> The corn grew five ells high in the stalk,
> The spike became five sixths of an ell . . .
> In my reign exuberance overflows,
> In my years abundance is heaped up.

The similarity between Hebrew poetry and Ugaritic poetry is most marked. In Hebrew the formal and precise parallelism has been developed in more ways than one, of which perhaps the most effective is the famous *qinah* rhythm (3:2), where the shortness of the second line gives a peculiar halting rhythm of a highly emotional type. This metre is used in lamentations (Hebrew *qinah*), but a beautiful example is to be seen in Psalm 23, which is all 3:2 rhythm except for verse 4. There we have three 2:2 lines instead of two 3:2 lines. Perhaps this is simply for the sake of variation, though it may be intended to express rising emotion. In Ugarit literature the parallelism is cruder and less developed, as though the writers found themselves bound to keep to the strict forms of parallelism, both in substance and in rhythm, without making any serious or sustained efforts in literary development. The Ugarit verse shows an earlier stage of development. Indeed this is only to be expected, since, apart from the barest of possibilities in respect of Judges 5, the latest Ugarit poem is earlier than the earliest extant Hebrew poem. Ugarit poetry represents substantially the kind of Canaanite-Syrian poetry which the Hebrews encountered when they entered the country. Apparently they took over everything—language, culture, poetic style and even the religion.

Here is an extract from the Anat-Baal poem cycle. It describes the Virgin-goddess Anat seeking permission from

Il, the chief god of the Ugarit pantheon, to build a house for Baal:

> Then she sets her face towards Il,
> At the courses of the Two Rivers,
> At the midst of the streams of the Two Deeps.
> She enters the abode of Il,
> And comes into the house of the King, the Father of
> Years.
> At the feet of Il, she bows and falls,
> Prostrates herself and honours him.

This type of rhythmical parallelism is found in couplet after couplet with an almost monotonous regularity, and no reader can fail to see that here we have the poetical style from which Hebrew psalmody developed. One noteworthy feature of the Ugarit poems is the use of consecutive numbers:

> Like the seven cries of his mouth,
> Yea, his eight shrieks.

or again,

> I will give her twice her weight in silver,
> Even thrice her weight in gold.

With these couplets, compare Hosea 6.2; Amos 1.3 etc.; Proverbs 30.21. There is a remarkable parallel in style to be seen in phrases of the type 'one day, two days', 'one place, two places', found in the Anat-Baal cycle, and the phrase 'one damsel, two damsels' of Judges 5.30, especially when we remember that the locality from which this Song Deborah comes is not very far removed from Ugarit itself. The Song cannot be far removed from Ugarit either in time or place. Another illustration is 'and the field, the field of the gods, the field of Asherat and Rachm'. This

is from the poem which has been entitled 'The Birth of
the Gods'. Compare 'Then did the horses stamp, by
reason of the prancings, the prancings of their strong ones',
Judges 5.22.

There are numerous points of contact between the
Ugarit texts and the Hebrew psalms, especially in respect
of metaphors and phrases. Some of these will be pointed
out in the particular psalms which will be dealt with later.
It is evident that the Hebrews took over practically the
whole of the Ugarit mythology, cleansing it of its polytheism
and its physical crudities of the sex-type, and reinterpreting
the ancient phrases. Psalm 82 seems to have been taken
over with a minimum of alteration. Verse 6 makes it clear
that the psalm really involves a judgment by El of gods and
not of men. El is the Hebrew equivalent of Il, the high
god of the Ugarit pantheon, and the name is used often of
JHVH as the High and Only God. Perhaps the most
intriguing connection between Hebrew psalms and Ugarit
texts is the persistence in Hebrew lore of the myth of the
fight against the Sea (*Yam*). This story of the fight of Baal
'the Rider of the Clouds' against the monster Yam is one
of the treasure finds of Ugarit, since this is a motif which
recurs again and again in Psalms and Prophets. Another
point of interest, though not for its association with the
psalms, is the function of the Virgin Anath, Mother of
the gods, whose duty it is to intercede with the High-
god Il.

But great as are the similarities, it is the differences that
matter most. Ends matter more than beginnings. Where
we start from is of much less account than where we are
going. Some of us, who have the right perspective, are not
worried about the apes out of which we seem to have
evolved, but we are very much concerned about what is
going to happen at the other end, whether men are going
to be gibbering dolts in a shattered world, or happy
sojourners in a world-garden of heart's desire. Nobody can
read the Ugarit texts side by side with the Hebrew psalms

without realizing that in literary style and phraseology they are very similar; but at the same time it is even more plain that religiously they are poles apart. The picture of the god Baal copulating with a heifer 'seventy and seven times; she is mounted eight and eighty times' has no parallel in the Hebrew psalms; neither is there any parallel, even in the most bloodthirstily patriotic psalms, to the picture of the goddess Anat wading up to her thighs in the blood of the slain. The Ugarit texts are polytheistic, with gods and goddesses acting in a most lustful and bloodthirsty manner, exhibiting all the passions and jealousies of men at the worst. The gods of Homer are bad enough, but they are patterns of propriety beside the Ugarit deities—though here it should be remembered that the Ugarit literature is much earlier than Homer, and Ugarit was destroyed at least a full century before the fall of Homer's Troy. Whilst there are many references to sacrifices in the Ugarit texts (for here we have the ground pattern of the Hebrew cultus: Amos was right in saying that this sort of thing was not known in the Wilderness), there is no reference to the necessity of true and right living as a basis for true sacrifice.

> She sacrifices seventy buffaloes,
> As an offering for Aliyn Baal,

and so on, couplet after couplet, seventy oxen, seventy head of small cattle, seventy head of deer, wild-goats, and (?) asses. It was this Canaanite multiplication of sacrifices against which the prophets and psalmists thundered. The Hebrew psalms, even when they contain such a survival as 82, speak of righteousness and justice, of humble devotion to a Saviour-God, and of the joy of the salvation which He provides. It is precisely here that the psalms differ from the Ugarit texts, and it is these religious elements that constitute the psalms as the Praises of Israel, making them still a manual of devotion, as much as three thousand years after some of them were written.

## (d) *Recent developments in the study of the psalms*

In recent years the tendency has been to study the psalms as the apparatus of a real and living cultus. A. C. Welch[5] believed that all the psalms were written for use in the temple ritual, some for public use and others for private use. This was also the view of J. P. Peters,[6] but the two scholars who have most influenced subsequent study along these and other lines have been Sigmund Mowinckel of Oslo and Hermann Gunkel of Berlin. Between 1921 and 1924, Mowinckel published six volumes of *Psalmenstudien*. He believes that the psalms originated in ritual needs, but thinks that some of them were largely potent spells which, when recited, released power. He thinks that the 'workers of iniquity', to whom frequent reference is made in the Psalter, were actually sorcerers, and that these particular psalms were recited by, or on behalf of, some individual who wished to be released from the binding power of a magic spell which had been fastened upon him. The same thing, he thinks, is true in the case of national psalms, which were recited to release the nation as a whole from spells which the enemy had bound upon it. Here Mowinckel is actually arguing on the basis of Meso-potamian psalms which are largely magical incantations intended for, and used to release, those who were suffering from sickness and misfortune from the spells which were the immediate cause of these troubles. This view propounded by Mowinckel has not met with much favour, but it has deserved more goodwill than it has actually received. It may well be that in the earlier stage of Hebrew religion there was a fair admixture of magic, and that men actually did think that the very recital of certain approved words was effective in the removal of all sorts of disabilities. Papyri from the first centuries B.C. and A.D. are full of this

[5] *The Psalter in Life, Worship and History*, 1926.
[6] *The Psalms as Liturgies*, 1922.

kind of thing. In some cases they amount to little more than a gibberish of outlandish names, apparently recited at great speed by the exorcist until one name proved effective and out the demon came. Ideas of this type are by no means dead, even in this 'civilized' world. It is quite probable that some of these ideas lingered on, just as many of the phrases and some of the motifs of the Ugarit myth-cycles survived. Once again, it is not a question of the similarities in phrase and so forth between Hebrew psalms and Mesopotamian incantations, but of those differences which have made the Hebrew psalms what they are. In any case, psalms which were originally incantations may, equally with ritual practices, have been retained largely in outer form, but reinterpreted to meet the growing awareness of the centuries. Some 'workers of iniquity' may have been sorcerers, but most of us can manage to work iniquity without the assistance of incantations and magic spells.

There is another theory of Mowinckel's, one which has received considerable support, and at present, with modifications due to the new Ugarit finds, seems to be well on the way to securing universal support. Mowinckel based this theory also on our knowledge of Babylonian religion, in this instance the annual accession festival (*akitu*-festival) of the Mesopotamian urban cults. The king received anew at the new year his sovereignty over the country, this being given back again to him by the tutelary god of the city, which in the sixth century B.C. Babylon of Nebuchadrezzar's time was Marduk. There was a ritual combat in which the god was represented as overthrowing his enemies once again, after which he reascended his throne to fix the fate for the following year and thus to declare his sovereign will. Some say there was a sacred marriage, wherein the king played the part of the god in company with a chosen representative of the goddess. Some say the god dies and comes to life again, but there was certainly a procession in which the image of the god was escorted to his royal judgment throne. Mowinckel maintained that in pre-exilic times the Ark, the symbol of the Presence of the God of Israel, was carried in some such similar procession, and that the psalms central to this new year ritual, of which they formed the liturgy, were 47, 93, 95-100, together with some forty other psalms which were associated with the ceremonies to a lesser degree. After the Exile, there was an arkless variant. The Ras-Shamra (Ugarit) texts have provided material of an agricultural rather than an urban pattern, and many who formerly viewed Mowinckel's theory with reserve are beginning to turn with favour towards his suggestions, though with the Ugarit pattern substituted for his Babylonian ground-scheme. There still is lack of definite evidence that there was an annual Coronation ceremony of this type in Israel or in Judah. Further, it is unlikely that 95-100 belong, in anything like their present form, to pre-exilic times. Psalms 47 and 93 may well contain early elements, and that part of 96 which is paralleled in 29 is early, whilst the theophany of 97 is a survival, so far at least as the phraseology is concerned, from ancient times. It is much more likely that, as we have suggested earlier, 93-99 were originally Sabbath psalms of the early post-exilic period. Mowinckel's theory, however, especially with modifications due to the Ugarit materials, is not dependent for its soundness on these particular psalms, and there is no doubt but that future study of the Psalter will have much to say concerning the relation of the Psalter to the annual Autumn Feast.

The work of Gunkel was a development of earlier work by W. Staerk and R. Kittel. He published a summary of his work on the classification of psalms in a composite volume entitled *Old Testament Essays* (1927), pp. 118-142, a volume containing papers read at a meeting of the Society for Old Testament Study held at Oxford in September, 1927. There are summaries of Gunkel's theories as to types (*Gattungen*) of psalms in two books, one published in 1938 in New York, the author being James Fleming and the title *Thirty Psalmists*, and the other, also published in New York, but in 1950, written by John Paterson, and entitled

*The Praises of Israel.* Gunkel held that there are four main classes of psalms: National Hymns of Praise, Private Hymns of Thanksgiving, National Hymns of Sorrow, Private Hymns of Sorrow. The thanksgiving hymns are older than the laments, and the national elements are older than the individual elements. The simpler the psalm is in structure and character, the earlier it is. Some psalms have elements common to more than one class. These he called *Mischgattungen* (mixed types). There are in addition various other types of psalms, some of them represented by one or two psalms only. These other types are Royal Psalms, Blessings and Curses, Pilgrim Psalms, Legends, Law Psalms, Prophetic Psalms and Wisdom Psalms.

The first group of national hymns of praise include the Songs of Zion, in praise of the Holy City, namely 46, 48, 66, 84, 87, 122. Another sub-group comprises the Enthronement Psalms, the psalms which Mowinckel associated with his supposed Coronation Festival. The psalms of the national sorrow type are 44, 60, 64, 80, 83. The largest group is those which are individual laments, and these number about forty. There are thirteen individual thanksgiving psalms, 18, 30, 32, 34, first half of 40, 41, 66, 92, 100, 107, 116, 118, 138. It is the general opinion that Gunkel has applied his classification theory with characteristic German thoroughness, but that he has certainly made a considerable contribution to the study of the Psalter by his careful separation and identification of the various motifs which are to be found therein. Gunkel was inclined to date the psalms largely in the pre-exilic period, a tendency which has largely been followed in recent years, partly no doubt as a revulsion from the attitude of the latter half of the nineteenth century when Maccabaean days and even later times were much in fashion. The attempt to date individual psalms or even groups of psalms is a most difficult project, and not least because it is more than likely that there has been a considerable amount of revision during the centuries, and it cannot be guaranteed that any one psalm is in the condition in which it left the original author's hand.

We have given a general picture of the general problems of all the Psalms. Let us now turn to consider in turn some of the individual psalms, first some of the psalms which were once in the collection known as 'The Sons of Qorach's' and then some which were once in the collection known as 'Asaph's'.

# II

## Psalm 42-43

## EXILED FROM THE TEMPLE

THESE PSALMS were originally one psalm. This is partly to be seen in the fact that the metre is almost completely regular throughout the two psalms. It is the famous *qinah* metre, used particularly for lamentations, for which its peculiar halting 3:2 rhythm renders it most suitable. The unity of the two psalms is to be seen more clearly in the refrain

> Why cast–down, my–soul? : and–turbulent within–me?
> Wait–in–hope for God : for–still will–I–praise–Him,
> My–present full–salvation and–my–God.

This refrain occurs thrice, 42.5; 42.11; 43.5. In the first instance (42.5) a correction is needed to bring the refrain into line with the other two. The corrected refrain is actually found in the *Septuagint Codex Alexandrinus*, in the Syriac Version, and in a few Hebrew manuscripts. The psalm was extant in 'The Music-master's' as well as in 'The Qorachites'.'

The psalmist is exiled from the Temple (42.6 and 43.3 and 4). He longs once more to be there, and longs with desperate eagerness. Once, in the glorious by-gone days, he had led the procession at the Feast, that great autumnal New-Year Feast which marked the climax of the whole year, both agricultural and ritual. (The verb *dadah* (42.4, 'went' in

Revised Version) is rare in biblical Hebrew, but from later Hebrew we know that it means 'hop, trip, stumble' of tied birds struggling along, or of tiny children who can scarcely walk. When the verb is transitive, it means 'to walk' a baby who cannot stand alone, and thence generally 'to lead'. This last is the meaning here. He led the throng, not so much slowly as with those short hobbled steps which belong to the movement of dense crowds. The only other occurrence of the verb in the Old Testament is in Isaiah 38.15, 'I shall hobble along all my years.') This exiled leader longs to be back in the Temple once more. Perhaps he was a priest, but even if not, he was certainly a cult official of some eminent degree.

> As–a–hind craves for–the–water brooks,
> So do–I crave for–thee, O–God.

The Hebrew has 'my–*nepesh*', but although this word is regularly translated 'soul' in the English Versions, there is not one single case where it ever means 'soul' in the sense of an immortal part of man's nature. The word is used frequently in poetry, both in the Psalms and in the Prophets, as a fulsome way of saying 'I' or 'thou'. Here the word with its suffix 'my' is a poetic way of saying '*I* long', the inference being that the longing is deep-seated, an overpowering emotion.

The psalmist is speaking of the anxious craving for fellowship with God of the man who once has known that fellowship. Here his craving is directly associated with the worship of God in His sanctuary. Those people, then or now, who are lackadaisical about attendance at church have never known what it really means to worship God. The man who knows in his own personal experience something of the joy of fellowship with God is not lackadaisical about any opportunity of renewing that fellowship, whether it be in private devotions or in public worship. In the last resort no enticement to be present in church is of avail other than

that soul-hunger which can be fed only with the Bread of
Heaven. Such a man cannot keep away. His own soul-
hunger will drive him thither.

The psalmist cries 'I am thirsty for God, for the living
El' (verse 3). Some scholars would read instead 'for the
El of my life' as in verse 8, but the phrase there is probably
a marginal note which has been transferred to the text. It is
best to retain the Hebrew text with its idea of 'the living
God'. There is a somewhat similar phrase 'living water',
which occurs twelve times, especially Jeremiah 2.13 and
Jeremiah 17.13, 'Jehovah, the fountain of living waters'.
The idea is spiritualized in John 4.10f., in the teaching
which arises out of the story of the Samaritan woman whom
Jesus met at the well of Sychar: 'Whosoever drinketh of
the water that I shall give him shall never thirst; but the
water that I shall give him shall become in him a well of
water springing up into eternal life.' Or again, in Revelation 7.17, where 'the Lamb . . . shall guide them unto
fountains of waters of life'. It is impossible for anyone to
understand the depth of meaning in this metaphor who
has not lived in a drought-ridden country of seasonal rains.

He continues: 'When shall I be able to enter and see
the Face of God?' This was the original, but the vowels of
the Hebrew were altered by the ancient Jewish scholars.
This was done regularly out of reverence, in order to make
the Hebrew read 'to appear before God'. The change
was due to a growing horror of anthropomorphism. It was
influenced partly out of a real understanding of the supreme
splendour and holiness of God. But perhaps the scribes
were influenced mostly by such a passage of scripture as
Exodus 3.6, where Moses, confronted with the burning bush
which did not burn itself out, 'hid his face: for he was
afraid to look upon God'. Even more influential was Exodus
33.17-23, with what may be an almost vulgar anthropomorphism. Moses asked to see God's glory, but he is not
allowed to see God's face, 'for man cannot see me and live'.
And so God placed Moses in a narrow cleft, covered him

with His hand until He had passed by, and then removed His hand so that Moses could catch a glance of His back-parts in the moment of His passing out of sight. Samson's father, Manoah, was terrified because he and his wife had seen the Angel of God, a visible and temporary manifestation of God, until his wife told him to use his common sense. She pointed out to him, 'He would not have done all He has done for us, if He was going to kill us' (Judg. 13.22f.). Or again, when Elijah advanced to the opening of the cave on Mount Horeb, he covered his face with his cloak away from the sight of God (I Kings 19.13). In all these instances we have primitive notions which ultimately developed into the idea of the true Vision of God. Primitive religion all the world over is full of the thought of the terrible, deadly danger involved for men in any sort of contact with that which is 'holy', i.e. that which belongs to or is associated with the supernatural. But this primitive stage has already passed so far as even the earliest strands of the Old Testament are concerned. Already there is no *qodesh* (holiness) apart from Jehovah Himself. Holiness already has come to signify the sum total of His Nature, and the content of the idea of Holiness develops side by side with the truer and deeper understanding of God.

According to Rudolf Otto,[1] there are two components in the complex category 'holy', the 'numinous' and the 'rational'. The numinous is the external object which induces a feeling of dependence in man. Its elements are awefulness, overpoweringness, urgency and fascination. For Otto the rational component is the ethical. He points out that the non-rational element begins with 'demonic dread' as the first form of primitive religious consciousness, and passes through 'fear of the gods' to the 'Fear of God'. Religious experience grows out of 'inchoate emotions and bewildered palpitations of feeling', and 'out of shudder, a holy awe'. He writes here, of course, not of the experience of the individual, but of the development through the

---

[1] *The Idea of the Holy*, Eng. tr. 1924, p. 116.

millennia of the past. But when he speaks of the rational element in 'holy', he means its ethical content. In modern times we have tended to go astray in our ideas of Holiness in respect of Otto's non-rational element in that we have not followed him closely enough, in respect of the rational element in that we have followed him too closely. It is a grave loss to us that in recent years we have so largely humanized away the elements of awefulness, overpoweringness and urgency in our thought of God. It is a still more serious loss that, whilst we have rightly emphasized the ethical purity of the Holy One, we have allowed ourselves to interpret Holiness almost entirely in ethical terms. It is not that this emphasis ought to be lightened for one moment or to the slightest degree. There is more need for sound ethical teaching to-day than ever there has been. But we have allowed the Moral God to take primary place in our thought, whereas the supreme Christian fact about God is that He is the Saviour-God. First and always He is the Saviour-God, and this is essential in both Old Testament and New Testament. Christian ethics are not based on ideas of man's duty to man, as is the case with even the highest pagan ethics, but on God's attitude to man. The result of this is that in Christian ethics there is an overplus beyond what is commonly called moral. The important thing about Jesus of Nazareth is not that He was good and kind, but that He is God-made-man, dying for men. 'God was in Christ reconciling the world to himself.' 'Thou shalt call his name Jesus, for it is he that shall save his people from their sins.' Morality is not enough, and it is nothing short of paganism to suggest that there can possibly be for the Christian works of supererogation. To say that God is Holy, means that He is full of Awe, One before whom all men must bow in fear and wonder. It means also that He is a God of morality, whose demands on men involve cleanness of outward deed and equally of inward thought. But it means also that He is the Saviour-God, the God who in Christ came to seek and to save that which was lost.

There is another development, this time associated with the idea of ' seeing God '. It is the transformation from the fear of the terrible Unknown to godly reverence and loving trust in the presence of the only pure and altogether lovely One, who can be known by those who worship Him in lowly love and humble obedience. Our God is not the Unknowable. He can be known by all who love Him, though it is a knowledge that is personal rather than intellectual. The desire to ' see God ' (cf. Moses and this psalmist) is deep-seated in all who ' earnestly desire the greater gifts' (I Cor. 12.31). This sight of God is the blessedness of the pure in heart (Matt. 5.8). This phrase ' the pure in heart ' is, like most of the phrases in the Beatitudes, an Old Testament phrase (Psalm 73.1 R.V.; Psalm 24.4). Originally it was largely ritualistic in content, and it may even be a relic of days when representations of the god (gods) were legitimate everywhere. But at the hands of the prophets and the psalmists the phrase became metaphorical. In the New Testament it comes to be seen to be dependent on faith unfeigned (I Tim. 1.4f.). Whoever comes to God in faith (i.e. full trust, recumbency upon God), repentant, relying upon the merits of the Crucified, that man ' sees God '. By ' seeing ' we mean that consciousness of the Presence of God in daily life which is both the privilege and the joy of the converted. It is a sight that grows more and more clear with the growing light of prayer and full devotion of life until at last there comes the full noonday of the soul, and the full Vision of God is vouchsafed. This full sight, equally with the first sight of God, is the gift of the Holy Spirit, but we ourselves must always be watching and praying. By the careful culture of the soul in an ever deepening faith, perhaps here, but certainly hereafter, we no longer shall ' see in a mirror ' with all the distortions of our human frailty, but 'face to face' (I Cor. 13.12).

This ' seeing' of God is spiritual and not physical. It corresponds to the Hebrew verb *hazah* rather than to the more common verb *ra'ah*, and is the spiritual insight of the prophet rather than the ordinary sight of everyday. This latter sight belongs to the realm of the physical and the mental; the 'seeing' of God belongs to the realm of the spiritual. Here we need to remember the statement of Paul in I Corinthians 2.14, that 'the natural man receiveth not the things of the Spirit of God: for they are foolishness unto him; and he cannot know them, because they are spiritually discerned.' To Paul, the 'natural' man is the physical-mental-psychological man in contrast to the 'spiritual' man. It involves at root a different kind of knowledge. Here once more the Hebrew helps us, for the regular Hebrew word for 'know' belongs to the realm of personal experience rather than that of intellectual perception. For instance, when the Hebrew says that Adam *knew* his wife, the meaning is that he had sexual intercourse with her, that is, he entered into an intensely personal relationship with her. Whilst this, of course, is a special use of the word, yet it is true that the word could never have been so used unless it had this personal association. Or again, Psalm 1.6 says that 'the Lord knoweth the way of the righteous'. This does not mean that God knows every detail of the road the righteous is taking as if it were worked out on a map with all the various places and stages named. It means that God is personally acquainted with the road, and that there is never a step which the righteous man takes but that God is there. Here the knowledge is of companionship and personal guardian care. The idea of 'seeing' God belongs to this category, and the reference is to personal awareness of fellowship with Him.

To return to the psalmist: the greatest burden which he has to bear is the jeers of his neighbours, who are constantly taunting him with his loss of the sense of the Presence of God, his inability to worship at the holy shrine. Because of this, his tears have been his food day and night, but he holds on grimly and determinedly to his memories. He drenches his soul with the remembrance of the time when he led the milling throng to the House of God. The word *sak* (throng) means 'an interwoven mass'. And so once more the refrain.

In the second stanza (verses 6-11), the psalmist tells us where he is. He is in the Jordan country, away north by the peaks of Hermon, as far away from Jerusalem as he could be whilst still in Israelite territory. Mount Mizar is unidentified. Any suggestion must be pure guessing. Verse 7 gives a picture of the distress and the trouble which have well-nigh overwhelmed the psalmist. He is overwhelmed by waves of trouble (cf. Psalm 88.7). The picture is of God opening the great rain-channels of the sky, and of the psalmist being swamped in the breakers and the billows of the subsequent flood.

From–Deep–to–Deep echoes the–noise–of–thy–rain–spouts,
All–thy–breakers and–thy–rollers have–passed–over–me.

Here in the mention of the Two Deeps, we have an echo of the old mythology. In the Ugarit text No. 129[2] there is a description of the goddess Anat seeking the presence of the high-god El:

> Then she set (her) face towards El
> At the torrents of the rivers,
> The midst of the streams of the Two Deeps.

It is apparent that these Two Deeps form in some way the boundaries of the abode of El, because the goddess Anat has already been described as having sprung with her foot and left the earth. The echoing of the great deluge of waters is that caused by the torrents issuing forth from the heavenly abode of God, and not the tempestuous noise of waters surging to and fro on the earth.

Verse 8 (in the Hebrew, verse 9) bears every mark of being an insertion. It is not in that 3:2 *qinah* rhythm which is characteristic of the psalm. Indeed it is very diffi-

[2] Gordon's list, *Ugaritic Handbook*, 1947.

cult to make any sort of poetry of it, and none at all unless we regard 'a prayer to the God of my life' as a marginal note. Further, the Sacred Name JHVH is used, whereas elsewhere in these twin psalms either El or Elohim is used, the latter having been substituted for JHVH as is usual in the Elohist Psalter. As the verse now stands, the psalmist is reminding himself of God's *chesed*, a very proper and sensible thing for him to do.

This word *chesed* is used in the Old Testament almost wholly in association with the idea of a covenant. This, at any rate, is its characteristic and truly important use. It stands primarily for the proper relation which the two parties to a covenant ought to maintain each towards the other. It is not necessary that the two contracting parties should be of equal status. It can be used even of treaties where one party has had perforce to accept the terms imposed by the other. Such a treaty was that enforced by David on the defeated Ammonites, referred to by Solomon (II Sam. 10.1f.). It is used of the covenant between David and Jonathan where David's *chesed* towards Jonathan involves the promise not to wipe out Jonathan's house when David becomes king (I Sam. 20.14-16). When we turn to the covenant between God and Israel, we have by no means an agreement between equals. Israel's *chesed* towards God involves a humble, loyal devotion to Him alone, and the observance of the laws which He has laid down. The tragedy of Israel's history was that her *chesed* was like the morning cloud and the dew which quickly vanish when the sun grows hot (Hos. 6.4), and all the more quickly when, as they say in Texas in August, 'the sun got up hot this morning'. Instead of showing loyal devotion to God alone, Israel worshipped the gods of Canaan 'upon the hills, and under oaks and poplars and terebinths' (Hos. 4.13). Instead of doing what was right between man and man, they filled the land with murder, theft and adultery, with oaths they never intended to keep (Hos. 4.2). So much for Israel's faithfulness to the covenant in the pre-exilic days. In post-exilic days, when the Law became the rule of daily life and especially after the days of Nehemiah and Ezra, *chesed* came to stand for that full devotion to the Law in which the Pharisees delighted, and the *chasid* ('saint', 'holy one' in the Psalter) was the man who was faithful to the Law.

God's attitude to an Israel which was thus so persistently wayward was necessarily one of forbearance and mercy, that is, if any shadow of the covenant was to remain. Israel stood in daily need of forgiveness and mercy. This is why the regular translation in the Septuagint of the Hebrew *chesed* is *eleos* and in the Vulgate *misericordia*, with their equivalents of 'mercy, loving kindness' in the English Versions.[3] In the New Testament the equivalent is *charis* (Grace). This word stands for the marvellous condescension of God, His continual mercy and forbearance for sinful men. It was because of this that Christ died for us whilst we were yet sinners. This grace is full and undeserved; it is independent of any merits in the receiver. What is required of us is that we turn to God in humble repentance and faith. This grace is not general benevolence towards the whole human race. It is a special pent-up love for His own specially chosen people, but now, in Christ, with the middle wall of partition broken down. The picture is not of a wide plain with static water stretching as far as the eye can see, but a pent-up torrent sweeping along and continually spreading over the plain, deep and strong and irresistible. Incidentally, concerning the old question as to whether grace is irresistible, the whole discussion is vitiated because it is discussed as an academic question, abstracted from experience. It is not an academic question, and ought not to be discussed from any theoretical angle. If it is so discussed, then men are bound to get either the wrong answer or no answer at all. The question arises because I, for myself and in respect of myself, know very well in my own heart that grace must be irresistible so far as I am

[3] For further details, see my *The Distinctive Ideas of the Old Testament*, 4th edition, 1950, 94-130.

concerned, if ever I am to find a place in the Kingdom of
His Love. Every other man must write and speak for
himself and on the basis of his own experience. I write from
mine. I believe that every man who is aware of what God
has done for him, in doing for him what he cannot do for
himself, also feels that if it were not that God's grace is
irresistible, he would still be where he was before; that is,
lost. The Christian knows that he is 'saved by grace
through faith'. For him faith is 'a recumbency upon him
(i.e. Christ), as our atonement and our life, *as given for us*
and *living in us* and in consequence hereof, a closing with
him and cleaving to him'. He knows also in his own heart
that all is of grace. Grace belongs essentially to the sphere
of personal relations, and it does not exist as a thing-in-
itself. It cannot be abstracted or generalized from the
personal experience of the person who is talking. The
general proposition 'Grace is irresistible' makes no sense.
The true proposition is 'Grace has been irresistible for
me'.

The psalmist pours out his prayer to God, whom he calls
his 'crag', symbol of inaccessible safety. He cannot understand why God apparently has deserted him, so that he
walks alone in misery because of the jeers and the oppres-
sions of his enemies. He is bruised to the bone because of
the continual sneers which they direct against him. And
so, once more, the refrain.

The third stanza (Psalm 43) opens with a plea for justice.
The first verse, as it now stands, is not truly rhythmical,
and it has been suggested that the word 'God' should be
transferred to the end of the verse. This straightens up
the syntax of the verse, and also provides two excellent
*qinah* lines.

> Judge–me and–plead my–plea
> From–a–nation that–is–not–*chasid*,
> From–a–man–of deceit and–villainy
> Deliver–me, O–God.

It is precarious to try to fix a date for the origin of any
particular psalm or for any group of psalms, because there
is generally a marked absence of any historical allusions
which are in the least degree definite. Indeed, in all cases
of this kind, there must always be a large measure of sub-
jective judgment. It has always seemed to me that the
most likely occasion for the original setting of this psalm
is the troubled times of the latter part of the fifth century B.C.
On the basis of this suggestion, the psalmist was a Qorachite
priest or cult-official ejected by Nehemiah in his ruthless
policy of separating the Jews who claimed to be of pure
descent from those who were alleged by them to be of
mixed blood. These men were driven out into the Northern
Territory and were not allowed to worship in the Jerusalem
Temple. The psalmist is a convinced worshipper of
Jehovah, whatever others may say about him. Like the
Isaiah 63.16 (who may well have been one of his companions
in distress), he could say, ' For thou art our father, though
Abraham knoweth us not, and Israel doth not acknowledge
us.' He prays for justice and for deliverance from a nation
which claims that it is *chasid*, that is, faithful to the Law
and the Covenant. The psalmist maintains that this claim
is false. They are not *chasid*. This conviction of his is
not put forward as a bare statement of fact, but as a deliberate denial (so the syntax of the Hebrew). I think, too,
that during the interregnum between Nehemiah's second
visit to Jerusalem (*c.* 426 B.C.?) and Ezra's arrival (397 B.C.),
many of these exiles returned, so that Ezra found quite a
large and influential group who were against the separatist
policy (Ezra 9.1-3), amongst them this Qorachite. I think,
too, that in his anxiety to have access to the Temple worship,
he with his fellow Qorachites accepted the lowly position
of door-keepers, and that Psalm 84 is the joyful song of this
returned group of exiles, glad now to be able to be even a
door-keeper in the House of the Lord.[4] It is freely admitted

[4] For further details, see my *Studies in the Psalter*, 1934, pp. 11-21,
38-42.

that such a reconstruction is largely conjectural, as must be the case with almost any attempt to describe the history of these critical times, but this reconstruction does provide a fitting setting for these psalms.

The psalmist once more asks why God has thus spurned him, and his final prayer is that God will send out His own true light, thus to lead him home again, back to God's holy hill, His dwelling-place on earth. Then will the psalmist come to God's altar, to the presence of the High God who is his source of joy. 'Then will I rejoice and praise thee with the harp, O God.' The psalmist longs desperately to worship once more there at the Holy Shrine. To be away from the Temple is darkness. It is to be thirsty as the hind pines for water in the time of drought. This psalmist knows the necessity and the joy of worshipping God in God's Holy Place. The man who does not worship God at a particular place and at a particular time, ceases in the end to worship God anywhere. He who would be conscious of the Presence of God, must deliberately make use of the associations of hallowed places and hallowed times, in order that, not only that place and time, but every place and time may become doorways for the invasion of the Holy Spirit. More than this, he must build up associations in daily life, so that the common details of every day may likewise become the windows through which the light of God may pierce the soul. This can apply most easily to the modern counterparts of incidents and sayings related in the Gospels. Children playing in the streets and open places can speak to us of One who saw the children in the market-places of His own Galilee, playing at weddings and at funerals. The man who gets something in his eye on a windy day, can recall to us One who once spoke of two men meeting in the street, and one said to the other, 'Let me get that little speck of dust out of your eye,' and he had a whole plank in his own eye. Or the woman searching the house and looking for a coin which she has lost, baking day, and a score of other domestic happenings can make occasions for thoughts of Jesus. Each and every common incident can become a means of opening ear and eye and heart to the presence of the living God. There are those perhaps who can spend the hours in continuous meditation, but most of us must busy ourselves with the hewing of wood and the drawing of water, and if we are to make anything of what we are doing, we must give our whole attention to the matter in hand. But, when we have built up a whole series of spiritual mnemonics, we can grow more and more into that life which is hid with Christ in God. The crown and core of this is going with the throng to the House of God. There the rich associations of our own past experiences and of the accumulated experience of saints of other days can be the means by which the doorways of the soul are kept fastened back lest the press of daily duties close the door.

The story of Bethel can speak to us here. It opens with a young man leaving home for the first time with a long desert journey in front of him. He was benighted at Luz, and there, with a stone for a pillow, he dreamed. He saw visions of God. This is not the only time that a hard pillow has proved itself to be the place on which there may rest the foot of a ladder that reaches up to heaven. The young Jacob saw God, and he vowed a vow that the God who had appeared to him there would be his God, wherever he might wander. He turned the stone up on end, consecrated it, and named that place Beth-El, House of God. Years after, as the order of the stories of Genesis would have it, Jacob passed that way again. This time he was in the throes of great anxiety, for two of his sons, Simeon and Levi, had treacherously attacked Shechem with fire and rapine. Jacob was afraid lest the friends of the murdered Shechemites should seek revenge. In his extremity of fear, he went to Bethel once more, and there he raised an altar to the God who had answered him in the day of his distress. Perhaps Genesis 35 is actually a variant of the other story in Genesis 28, though both stories are said to have traces of the

E-tradition. In any case, Jacob found new courage and strength, and Bethel once more was House of God to him in his time of need. Bethel was Jacob's shrine, his meeting place with God. For centuries Bethel was a sacred place for the descendants of Jacob. The priest there would tell these ancient tales for the edification of the worshippers. These visitors would then the more easily find that strength and help which they came to seek, aided by the memories of their own repeated visits. Strange things were done in Bethel during its long history, and rites were observed there which earned the disapproval of the prophets, but men did find God there, and there are some who maintain that later Jewish religion owes at least as much to Bethel as to Jerusalem itself. Bethel is a great name, as many wayside chapels testify. It stands for the sacred place where men may eat the food of angels, and eating there may find heavenly food on earthly platters. But there is no food of the soul to be found on earthly platters unless men have trained themselves to eat by faith at heavenly tables.

# III

*Psalm 44*

# THE WRONG TURNING

THIS PSALM is composed of twenty-six 3:3 couplets in three stanzas. The first stanza (verses 1-8) tells the story of God's mighty deed of olden time; the second stanza (9-16) recounts the psalmist's present distress; the third stanza (17-24) declares the psalmist's innocence of the charges of apostasy which have been levelled against him and are the source of his distress. The last two couplets may be part of the original psalm, or they may be an addition. It is difficult to decide on this matter. Doubtless many of the psalms have received additions and modifications during the generations of their use, just as is the case with many of the hymns we use to-day. Every minister of the gospel knows from experience how dangerous it is to use different editions of hymn books in a church service. Sometimes the number of verses is different, sometimes the order of the verses, and usually there are differences in the text. The first two couplets are:

O–God, with–our–ears we–have–heard,
Our–fathers have–recounted to–us
The–Deed thou–didst in–their–days,
(which) In–days–of–yore thy–hand performed. (v.1).

The last line involves a conjectural emendation which straightens out the metre, elsewhere studiously observed.

47

The rhythm has lapsed at the end of verse 1 and at the
beginning of verse 2, making the syntax difficult also. An
easier emendation is:

> (which) In–days–of–yore thou (didst) with–thy–hand
> (i.e. by thy power).

The psalm continues

> Nations thou–didst–dispossess and–didst–plant–them,
> Peoples thou–didst–ruin, and didst–make–them–spread.
> (v. 2).

The Authorized Version, followed by the margin of the
Revised Version, translates the end of the last line 'cast
them out', taking both verbs in the line to refer to the
nations of Canaan. But the last verb in line 2 actually
parallels the last verb in line 1, so that the 'them' of both
lines refers to the incoming Israel. This is probably the
intention of the Revised Version, but it is not as clearly
expressed as is desirable.

The figure employed is that of the vine. God planted
Israel as a true vine in the land which He had cleared, and
the new vine flourished, sending out its branches far and
wide. The excellence of the figure depends upon the understanding of the culture of the vine, whereby the branches
are cut down to the stock when once the vintage is over, so
that in the spring the new fruit-bearing branches grow again
with a vigour that is remarkable, and in some varieties to a
very great length. The same figure is used in the Asaphite
psalm 80.8-16, where verses 8 and 9 make the meaning here
plain. In 80.11 the branches reach out to the Mediterranean
on the one side and to the River Euphrates on the other, the
idealized eastern and western boundaries of the Messianic
Kingdom of David and his heirs.

This figure of the vine is one of the favourite figures for
Israel in the Bible, largely because of the allegory of

Isaiah 5.1-7, though in such a land such a metaphor is natural. Our Lord Himself certainly had this allegory of Isaiah's in His mind when He told the parable of Matthew 21.33-41. He opened His story with the same details, the hedge, the winepress and the tower. It would therefore be clear from the beginning of the story what the reference was, since the chief priests and the elders of the people would remember very well that 'the vineyard of the Lord of Hosts is the house of Israel, and the men of Judah the plant (i.e. the vine which God had planted) of his delight'. The same figure is used in Jeremiah 2.21 and 12.10, by Ezekiel in 17.1-10, and again in Joel 1.7. In Herod's Temple there was a huge golden vine, the symbol of Israel, hanging over the porch before the Holy of Holies, and so situated that it could be seen through the eddying smoke of the sacrifices. The clusters of grapes are said to have been as large as a man. But particularly, the figure of the new shoot growing out of the old stock is used often in references to Messiah. The apparent deadness of the old gnarled stock, with the new branches almost leaping out from it with the warmth of the spring, is most impressive. Nothing can seem more dead than the vine stocks which many English visitors can see in winter or in spring in those vineyards on the hillsides between Lausanne and Montreux, and there are few plants which show more vigour when once the warmer weather comes. Messiah is the Branch (*netser*), Isaiah 11.1. He is the Shoot (*tsemach*), Isaiah 4.2; Jeremiah 23.5, 33.15; Zechariah 3.8, 6.12; or the twig-branch (*choter*), Isaiah 11.1 which springs with renewed life from the ancient stock of Jesse. He is David's line, reborn and vigorous with new life. There can be no doubt but that the allegory of the True Vine in John 15.1-5 is a Messianic declaration and claim.

There are three Old Testament passages which have close affinities, and can well be discussed together. They are Psalm 44; Isaiah 63.7—64.12; and Psalm 78. All three passages tell of God's saving mercies of olden time, of His

choice of Israel, of Israel's persistent waywardness, and of
Israel's final rejection.  The first two passages deny the
charges of apostasy, and pray desperately that God will
turn again towards them, that He will relent from having
cast them off.  Psalm 78, on the other hand, regards the
rejection of Ephraim as final.  Ephraim-Israel has ceased
to be the People of God.  Judah has come to be the Chosen
One.

Isaiah 63.7f. tells of God's continued mercies (*chesed*) to
the House of Israel.  He said, ' Nay, but my people are they,
sons who will not deal falsely,' and that is why He was
their Saviour.  He saved them in spite of repeated rebellion,
brought them through the sea, dividing water before them,
and at last led them into Canaan the land of rest, just as
the herdsman brings his cattle down into the valley.  But
everything now has gone wrong.  Abraham-Israel will have
nothing to do with the writer and his friends.  They deny
that the psalmist and his company have any right to call
upon Jehovah (verse 16).  The writer says : ' We are become
"From of old thou didst not rule over them: thy Name
was not given them (lit. ' thy name was not called over
them ')".'  They never, so their adversaries say, had any
right to be called the People of God, and they have therefore been cast out as alien apostates.  They vigorously
protest (Isa. 64.8).  They say with great emphasis that
Jehovah is their Father; they are the clay and He the potter.
They are all of them His people.  And so they pray for a
reversal of fortune.

This is the general tenor of Psalm 44.  The psalmist
likewise has been charged with ' dealing falsely ' (verse 17;
cf. Isa. 63.8) in the covenant.  He deliberately denies that
he has been to any degree an apostate.  He too tells of God's
goodness in the early days, how God brought them into
Canaan, gave them the land, and prospered them.  The
psalmist is conscious of being cast off among the heathen,
a scorn and a derision to those amongst whom he is
dwelling.

The conclusion is natural that Psalm 44 and Isaiah 63.7—64.12 are from the same group of people, men who were alleged by their enemies to belong to a wayward, apostate section of Israel, but men who vigorously deny that they are apostates. The crimes with which they are charged are those which are repeated again and again in Deuteronomy (4.9; 4.23; 4.28; 6.12, etc.), and these are the charges which are levelled by the southerners against the northerners in II Kings 17, the chapter which contains the southern charges against those whose descendants came to be called Samaritans. Psalm 44 belongs to the same general situation as Psalm 42-43, as well as to that of Isaiah 63.7ff. Both psalms and the section from the Prophet reflect the rivalries of north and south, and form the northerners' protest against what they believe to be the harsh treatment which has been meted out to them.

The contrast, and the other side of the story, is to be found in Psalm 78, where we find all the charges which Psalm 44 and Isaiah 63.7ff. deny. Psalm 78 tells the story of God's continued love and forbearance and of His people Israel's continued waywardness. Ephraim, the warriors of the Lord who fought for Him the battle of Canaan, failed in the day of battle. They conquered the territory, but conquering Canaan meant more than conquering territory. In the end it was Canaan that conquered them. The Israelites did not keep the covenant. They refused to obey His Law. They followed the ways of Canaan.

The psalmist tells the story of Ephraim's continued waywardness from the beginning. God brought them out of Egypt, made a pathway for them through the sea, led them through the desert, cloud by day and column of fire by night. He clave the rock of Rephidim for them, and gave them angels' food to eat. He forgave their persistent apostasy in the desert, and finally brought them into the land of Canaan. But there in Canaan, the old tale of waywardness and apostasy was re-enacted, worship at the pagan shrines with their idolatry and their immoralities. First Shiloh, the original home of the Ark, was abandoned, and at last Israel was taken away captive, rejected and lost. 'He rejected the tent of Joseph, and chose not the tribe of Ephraim.' The choice turned over to David, to Judah and to Mount Zion. It is to be noted that the psalmist of Psalm 44 and the writer of Isaiah 63.7ff. have the same charges levelled against them as Psalm 78 levels against Ephraim, but all of them cling to Jerusalem as their spiritual home. We have, therefore, to assume that the group represented by Psalm 44 and the Isaiah passage were classed with the northerners, with them but not of them. This is why we have supposed that they were the men who were driven out of Jerusalem as a result of the reforming zeal of such men as Nehemiah and Ezra.

The assumption is sometimes made that the Hebrews were more religious naturally than any other people, and that herein is the reason for God's choice of them to be His special people. All the evidence goes to show that this so-called genius for religion was confined to a very small group, namely the canonical prophets and those few who listened to them. The people as a whole were wayward. They were not more wayward than other peoples; their crime was that they were not less wayward. They persistently turned aside from the worship of the One True God. The charge is not that they were more irreligious than their neighbours. The charge is that they were indistinguishable from them. It was but a small minority who were different and were faithful to Jehovah alone. A short summary of the internal evidence for this is given in Psalm 78, but there is an increasing body of evidence external to the Old Testament. We proceed to give illustrations of this.

First, there is the evidence from the Jews of Egypt in the sixth-fifth centuries B.C. These Jews lived at Elephantine, an island close by the first cataract of the Nile. It was the farthest point south reached by Herodotus in his travels. The Egyptian name was Yeb, and these Jews formed a military garrison, whose duty was to guard Egypt against an Ethiopian invasion from the south. Probably it was the

Assyrians who first instituted this military post, but Herodotus tells us that the Persians maintained a garrison there. The native Pharaohs evidently continued the practice after the Persians had been driven out. These Jews had built a temple there sacred to Jahu (an ancient spelling, probably, as we think, the correct one), but they had provided him with two wives, Anath and (probably) Ashimah. There are five different names mentioned in the papyri which have been found, but they are reducible to these three. Anath is the Queen of Heaven, wife of Anu, one of the great early triad of Babylonian gods. She was worshipped in North Syria, where her regular title was The Virgin Anat. In these Ugarit texts she is mostly the consort of Baal, though sometimes of El. Indeed there is everywhere in these texts confusion between Anat, Astarte and Asherah. Anath left her name in Palestine: at Anathoth, where Jeremiah was born; in two place names, Beth-anath in Judah and Beth-anath in Galilee. In Jeremiah 7.18 we find a picture of the whole of the Jerusalem population zealously worshipping the Queen of Heaven; and twenty-odd years later we find the Jews who had fled to Egypt after the murder of Gedaliah, defending their cult of the Queen of Heaven on the amazing ground that when they worshipped her in the old days, all went well (Jer. 44.16-18), and that, said they, is why they refused to listen to what Jeremiah had to say to them in the Name of Jehovah. Apparently it was not only the northerners who were apostate, for whilst the Elephantine Jews probably were of northern origin, these other Jews, who refused to listen to the prophet Jeremiah, were certainly southerners.

Ashimah is mentioned in II Kings 17.30 amongst the deities who were worshipped by those settlers in North Israel who were introduced by the Assyrians after the collapse of the northern kingdom. It is more than likely that she was known there before that time, because Amos 8.14 should probably read, 'Ye who swear by the Ashimah of Samaria.' The fact that at Elephantine Jehovah should have two wives is not as surprising as might at first sight appear. The custom of a chief wife and a secondary wife is recognized as being legal in Deuteronomy 21.15-17, and even in Leviticus 18.18, this latter being a post-exilic Priestly Code passage, where two wives are admissible provided that they are not sisters. There is therefore a fair amount of evidence to support the contention that this particular type of polytheism was imported by the Jews who went to Egypt from Palestine. It is not natively Egyptian. But the astonishing thing is that there is extant amongst the Elephantine texts a copy of a letter written to the authorities at Jerusalem, dated *c*. 408 B.C., and this letter shows that the Elephantine Jews were 'in communion' with the officials there.

Further disconcerting evidence is the south Palestinian coin, probably from Gaza, now preserved in the British Museum. The coin dates from *c*. 400 B.C. On the reverse side of the coin there is a figure of a male bearded god, sitting on a winged car. The god is a solar Zeus, but with suggestions of the vegetation deity Triptolemus, worshipped as the inventor of the plough. The name of the god is written on the coin in Aramaic lettering, and that name is Yahu, spelt as at Elephantine and one of the ancient ways of writing the Divine Name. This is syncretism, and whatever exactly may be the origin of the coin, it is certain that the cult was sufficiently official in south Palestine for the coin to be struck.

Let us turn back to the internal evidence as it is lit up by recent archaeological discoveries. In II Kings 1 the story is told of how king Ahaziah of Israel fell through the lattice of an upstairs room of his palace in Samaria and was seriously injured. He sent messengers to the oracle of 'Baalzebub god of Ekron' to learn whether he would recover from his injuries. These messengers were intercepted by Elijah, who sent them back post-haste to the king with the question, 'Is it because there is no god in Israel, that thou sendest to inquire of Baalzebub the god of

Ekron?' It is many years since it was suggested that Baal-zebub (Lord of dung-hill flies) was a mocking change by the copyists for the true name Baal-zebul. We know now that this latter is the name of the life-god of Syria. This fact enables us to see clearly what Ahaziah was doing. The whole incident is clear evidence of the way in which the Ephraimite north became entangled with the Canaanite cults, which were closely similar to those portrayed in the Ugarit texts, so strong in the land when the Israelites invaded the country, and still strong in the ninth century.

This brings us to Elijah on Mount Carmel. It has always been assumed that the fight there was against the cult of Baal-Melkart, god of Tyre, introduced by Jezebel, the Tyrian princess who came to marry Ahab of Israel. It may well be that she brought with her some special features of the Tyrian cult, but the god at root is the Syrian Baal. His name appears everywhere in the Ugarit texts. He is Prince Baal, the Rider of the Clouds, and it is he, the texts say, who brings the rain and gives fertility to the parched land. Elijah was not fighting merely against a Tyrian deity introduced by a foreign princess. He was fighting against the ancient cult of Canaan, those old gods who still lived on in the devotion of the people of the north. The Book of Deuteronomy is quite right in its steady repetition of charges and warnings concerning the gods of the peoples who were round about them. The fact is that the religion of the north was riddled through and through with the cults of Canaan. The bull set up at Bethel may have been a revival of the desert cult of the Golden Calf. It is more likely that it was the bull of El, the High-god of Syria. He was worshipped in the form of a bull, and the title Bull-El occurs again and again in the Ugarit texts.

Further, it is commonly said that the northerners were confusing Jehovah and Baal. I wonder whether this was really the case? It is more likely that they had equated Jehovah with El (Il), and that whereas the native Ugarit-Canaanite custom involved the worship of El and Baal, the new variation was the worship of Jehovah-El and Baal. This would account for the fact that Ahab could favour the cult of Baal-Hadad-Melkart and at the same time give his sons names of which the divine name Jahu formed a part, e.g. Ahazyahu and Jehoram.

The prophets, then, were saying nothing less than the truth when they remonstrated with the Israel of the north. The cults of the Syrian-Canaanite gods were everywhere, on every hill and in every city and town. Everywhere there was idolatry and sacred prostitution. Not one line of their picture is overdrawn. God's choice of Israel to be His ' peculiar ' people was certainly not based upon any monotheistic intuition or religious genius of the people. Israel is regularly and rightly represented as choosing other gods as well as Jehovah, and other things than those in which He delights. With the Assyrian domination of Syria in the eighth century and on into the seventh century, the situation grew worse, because then the astral cults of the Assyrian star-gods were introduced (Amos 5.26) to supplement the original paganism of the land. Deuteronomy 7.7 and the kindred passages are right. It was not because of anything in Israel that God chose Israel.

Why, then, did God choose Israel? Or, having rejected Israel, why did He choose Judah? Psalm 78 gives no clue to the answers to these questions. It gives reasons for God's rejection of Ephraim, but not for God's original choice of them. No reason is given for His subsequent choice of Judah. But, before an answer is attempted to the question *Why* did God choose Israel, it is better to ask and to attempt to answer another question first: *When* did God choose Israel? There are two answers given to this question in the Old Testament. They were first brought into prominence in a monograph by Kurt Galling, published in 1928 and entitled *Die Ehrwählungstradition Israels.*

The first answer is that of pre-exilic Israel. It is the answer of the prophets. They link the choice closely with the deliverance from Egypt. Alternatively, the choice was in the desert and concerned the occupation of Canaan. This alternative is found in Deuteronomy 32, Ezekiel 16, and in the Qorachite psalms. It is curious that these passages do not refer to the Exodus itself. Apparently there was a tradition which did not make much of the Exodus from Egypt, and passed it by in favour of the desert journeys. The second answer to the question *When?* is the mainly post-exilic answer, and it is to be found predominantly in the Priestly Code. Both answers were sound in that in each case the whole initiative was realized to be God's. He chose them; they did not choose Him. Parallel with this, in the non-Exodus tradition, is the acknowledgment that the occupation of Canaan was His work and not theirs.

For–it–was not–by–their–sword (that) they–inherited
   the–land,
And–their–arm did–not–save them.
But (it was) thy–right–hand and–thy–arm
And–the–light–of thy–presence, because–thou–didst–
   favour them.
Thou–indeed art–my–king and–my–God,
Determining victories for–Jacob. (44.3-4).

In practice, however, the two answers worked out very differently. The first answer, with its datum-line as the Exodus, continued to insist that everything depended upon the work of their Saviour-God. The God, who of old time and at the beginning of their history as a nation brought them up out of Egypt and settled them in Canaan, was still their Saviour, 'still commanding victories for Jacob'. What was required of Israel was 'to do justly, to love mercy (*chesed*, i.e. to delight in being faithful to the covenant), and to walk humbly before God'. The second answer with its references to the patriarchs grew in time to have exactly the opposite effect. Ultimately it worked out that the emphasis was put on the fact that they were the sons of the patriarchs, and that the promises made to the patri-

archs were to be fulfilled in them because they were the sons
of the patriarchs. This involved them in relying upon what
they themselves were, and not trusting wholly in God.
They forgot that salvation, then and now, is by grace
through faith, and only by God's grace.

In illustration of the pre-exilic answer that God's choice
of Israel was linked with the rescue from Egypt and the
settlement in Canaan, we refer to the following passages:
Amos 3.1-2; Hosea 13.4; Hosea 2.2-23; Jeremiah 2.3f.;
Ezekiel 20.5ff. and of course, our three writings, Psalms 44
and 78, and Isaiah 63.7ff. Psalm 78 belongs to the pre-exilic
period before the destruction of the Jerusalem Temple and
the disaster of the exile. The other two writings belong to
the exilic or the early post-exilic period. The earlier strands
in the Pentateuch tell the same story. A most noteworthy
example is the Ten Commandments. They begin (Ex.
20.1-3) with, 'And God spake all these words, saying: I
am the Lord thy God, which brought thee out of the land
of Egypt, out of the house of bondage.' Israel, that is, is
commanded to acknowledge Jehovah as God because He
brought them up out of Egypt. This is the reason why
Israel is to have no other gods. This is the reason why
Israel must keep the Commandments. It is not because the
Commandments are right, nor because they are a sound
basis for society, whether nomadic, agricultural or urban.
The real reason is given quite definitely: God was their
Saviour, and He brought them up out of the land of
Egypt. Herein, incidentally, is the fundamental difference
between Hebrew-Old Testament-New Testament religion
and a great deal of modern 'Christian' thought which has
taken over Greek ideas as a basis, and would give other
reasons as to why man must live a moral life. The same
salvation motif can be seen even in the incident of the
molten calf. The reason which was produced for the
institution of the cult was, 'These be thy gods, O Israel,
which brought thee up out of the land of Egypt' (Ex. 32.4).
This cry was repeated when Jeroboam son of Nebat set up

the golden calves at Bethel and at Dan (I Kings 12.28). The knowledge that the salvation motif is paramount was so imbedded that even when they committed the greatest crime against Jehovah (the Golden Calf was reckoned to be the height of apostasy), they still maintained that motif.

So long as the Hebrews kept on asking *When* God chose them, they managed to get substantially the right answer. The trouble began when they started to ask the wrong question. It was then that they began to get the wrong answer. It usually is. In religion certainly, and probably for everything else, the problem of man is not so much to find the right answer, as to ask the right question. At any rate, as soon as the Hebrews began to ask *Why* God had chosen them, forthwith the trouble began.

In Psalm 44.3, they still have the right answer. It is because He had 'a favour unto them'. The Hebrew verb here is *ratsah*. This root has mostly to do with God's good favour, that supreme generosity of His which springs directly out of His Nature, that full forgiveness which He freely grants to the truly repentant who are willing to do what they can to make amends. It stands for God's pardon and for the consequent restoration of fellowship with Him. The verb is used in Isaiah 40.2, where the Revised Version has 'her iniquity is pardoned', and the margin 'her punishment is accepted'. The meaning is that Jerusalem has paid the full penalty for her sin, and that, turning back to God in full repentance, she is received back into her original relationship with God. The root is used generally of God's appreciation of man's sincere efforts towards reconciliation with Him. These efforts must consist of true repentance with a sincere desire to make amends, all based on a full reliance upon Christ, trusting in His redeeming grace. Half the trouble in religion has been due to the fact that men have thought that there are other conditions for reconciliation with God which men must fulfil, such as strict observance of rituals, or good works, and so forth. The noun *ratson* (goodwill) is used only of

God Himself, except in Genesis 49.6 and in late contexts. To secure this *ratson* (God's goodwill) is the whole aim of true religion, for there is nothing worthy to be compared to a man's being in the right relationship with God, and equally there is nothing at all that can compensate for the lack of it. All this needs particularly to be remembered in connection with the Angels' Song in Luke 2.14. The phrase 'men of goodwill' is used regularly of good fellowship and a sweet reasonableness between man and man. The phrase means nothing of the sort, as the paraphrase of the Revised Version has sought to show, with its 'Peace among men in whom he is well pleased'. The Greek word here is *eudokia*, and it stands for the Hebrew *ratson*. The line therefore means that peace comes on earth to men who are right with God. Man can never be right with man unless man is first right with God. Perhaps there will come a day when men of affairs generally will realize this. Until that day we must continue to stagger from one crisis to another, propped up by pious exhortations to increased moral efforts.

The beginnings of trouble amongst the Hebrews appear already in the J-tradition in Genesis 18.19. This occurred when another answer was suggested to the question *When?* 'For surely I have known him (i.e. Abraham), that he may command his children and his household after him, that they may keep the way of the Lord, to do justice and judgment, to the end that the Lord may bring upon Abraham that which he hath spoken of him.' The point here is that the time of the choice is taken away back behind the Exodus, back to Abraham. It is as well to notice also that there is also raised in this verse the matter of statements made to Abraham which must be fulfilled, because it was as a development of this as much as in any other way that the wrong answer came with all the woe it brought to Jewry. The same situation can be seen in Joshua 24.2ff., a passage which is usually ascribed to the E-tradition. Joshua is represented as saying: 'Your fathers dwelt of old time beyond the river (i.e. Euphrates), even Terah the father of Abraham and the father of Nahor: and they served other gods. And I took your father from beyond the river and led him throughout the land of Canaan . . .' and so on, with the rescue from Egypt, the journey through the desert, the settlement in Canaan, all the old motifs, the difference once more being that the story is taken back to Abraham.

The other question, *Why* did God choose Israel? is first asked in Deuteronomy, especially in Deuteronomy 7.7, the *locus classicus* for the choice of Israel. 'The Lord did not set his love upon you because ye were more in number than any people, for ye were the fewest of all peoples. But because the Lord loveth you, and because he would keep the oath which he sware unto your fathers, hath the Lord brought you up with a mighty hand, and redeemed you out of the house of bondage from the hand of Pharaoh, king of Egypt.' Here we get two answers to the question *Why?* The first is: It was all because God loved them. This is the answer given in Psalm 44.3, and it is the right answer. It is the only answer which does not bring disaster. The second answer arises out of the attempt to get behind that great act of salvation, 'the Deed which thou didst in their days, in the days of old', the rescue from Egypt and/or the settlement in Canaan. The second answer was that it was because of the oath which He sware to the patriarchs. We find the same reference to 'their fathers' in Deuteronomy 10.15 and again in 4.37. This reference is very common in Deuteronomy, and is in fact one of the characteristic phrases of the book. There are nearly fifty such references, and most of them are concerned with this oath which God sware to the fathers, the oath which He fulfils in His loving-kindness towards the Israel of the day.

So long as the emphasis continued to be on God's part in the matter, the idea of the choice being extended away back to the patriarchs did no particular harm. Indeed it was all to the good. The reference was sound because it laid an increased emphasis on the reliability of God and His faith-fulness. For instance, the passage which has just been quoted continues: 'Know therefore that the Lord thy God, he is God, the *faithful* God, which keepeth covenant (*berith*) and mercy (*chesed*) with them that love him and keep his commandments to a thousand generations.' It says 'the faithful God' and 'to a thousand generations'. This is splendid. It means that God's salvation of Israel at the Red Sea or His making a place for them in Canaan, was no mere flash in the pan, no sudden impulse, nothing done on the spur of the moment, nor in any irresponsible fashion whatever. It was part of His very Nature. He is like that always—to a thousand generations. He chose their father Abraham in exactly the same way and for exactly the same reason. He brought him right across the eastern desert through Harran and along into the land of Canaan. Here we have an increased emphasis on the idea of faithfulness, reliability, and all the more enduring because of the longer story of it. The earlier idea had been that Israel came to be a nation at Sinai after Moses had been sent by Jehovah of the Bush to bring out of Egypt a collection of loosely organ-ized and thoroughly mixed tribes. Moses brought them to Sinai, and there they were welded into a people, but not just *a* people, it was into *the* people, the People of God. But now we are given to understand that the nationhood of Israel virtually goes back very much further, a thousand generations, so to speak. We get the same word 'faithful' coming up again in Isaiah 49.7, where once again the asso-ciation is with the choice of Israel. 'Kings shall see and arise (i.e. stand up in honour), princes and they shall prostrate themselves, because of the Lord who is faithful, the Holy One of Israel, for he hath chosen thee.' And, again, important for us as Christians, the same idea is taken up again in Hebrews: 'God, having of old time spoken unto the fathers in the prophets by divers portions and in divers manners, hath at the end of these days spoken unto us in his (Greek 'a') Son', and throughout the epistle

'faith' is trusting in these promises, relying upon this faithful God. These promises were fulfilled in part in every
hero of the faith (see chapter 11), but their true fulfilment
must include us also, for without us the promises cannot be
fully implemented. It is this element of emphasis on the
promises of the *faithful* God, the God upon whom men can
confidently rely, which links the faith of this epistle with
the faith of the writings of the apostle Paul.

The same reference to earlier time is found more than
once in Isaiah 40-55, but here the work of the faithful God
is carried right away back beyond even the patriarchs, away
back to the beginning of things: 'Who hath wrought it and
done it, calling the generations from the beginning? I, the
Lord . . .' (See also Isa. 42.9, 43.13, and especially 51.10,
where the reference is to the primeval time.) His mighty
saving acts in the history of Israel are linked up with the
Creation myth, the story of God's victory over the monster
of Chaos before the beginning of the world. This is better
and better. He has been like this from all eternity. The
reference in Revelation 13.8, 'The Lamb that hath been
slain from the foundation of the world', may be wrong
syntactically and exegetically (the reference is to the book
written and not to the Lamb), but it is certainly right
theologically and religiously.

But when they asked the question *Why* did God choose
us? the reference to Abraham proved to be their undoing.
The answer came to be: Because we are Abraham's children;
because we keep the covenant; because we keep the Sabbath;
because we are circumcised; because we make the proper
sacrifices; because we keep the Law. The evidence for this
is to be found: for circumcision, Genesis 17, verses 10, 11
and 13, where circumcision is both the sign of the covenant
and the covenant itself; for the Sabbath, Exodus 31, verses
16 and 17. All these references are in the Priestly Code.
The salvation motif has disappeared, and nothing of
God's saving work remains. The emphasis has come to
be on what Israel was and what Israel did. It has ceased

to be upon what God is and on what God has done for
them.

The first Israel, Ephraim-Joseph, was rejected because of
their waywardness. They copied the ways of Canaan, as
both Psalm 78 within the Bible and the modern excavations
without the Bible, make quite clear. And so, too, for the
second Israel, the tribe of Judah, whose choice by God
forms the conclusion of Psalm 78. They, too, fell away to
the worship of other gods beside Jehovah, the gods of
Canaan and the gods of Assyria. The third Israel, ' the
children of the captivity ' as they called themselves, made
very sure of not repeating the mistake of their forbears.
They made very sure indeed of not falling away into the
ways of the heathen. They built a wall around themselves.
They cast out all who could not show a pure descent, which
meant in practice all who could not trace their descent from
one of the returned exiles, and amongst those who were
cast out, there were, it would seem, the authors of the
Qorachite psalms 42-43 and 44 and the author of Isaiah
63.7ff. These returned exiles developed their institutions in
order that by them they could save themselves. Their very
institutions became the cause of their rejection. When God
came to save them from their institutions, they murdered
God.

The exact point at which they took the wrong turning
was not so much in respect of circumcision and Sabbath and
the rest of their rules and regulations, as in the fact that
they got their explanations exactly and precisely wrong.
They *ought* to have said: Because God saved us and has
been good to us, that is why we do these things. But they
*did* say: Because we do these things, that is why God will
save us and be good to us. If they had kept to Deuteronomy
6.20-22 in the spirit as well as in the letter, all might have
been well, but the fatal twist was already embodied in the
very same context in verse 24. The verses 20-23 are sound:
' When thy son asketh thee, What mean the testimonies,
and the statutes . . . then thou shalt say, We were Pharaoh's

bondmen in Egypt, and the Lord brought us out . . .' but verse 24 is 'the Lord commanded us to do all these things . . . that he might preserve us alive . . .'

Given the assumption that the emphasis was to be upon what they themselves did, the rest of the Pharisaic scheme follows quite logically. If you believe that it is what you do that ensures your salvation, if you believe, that is, that you are saved by your own works, then the obvious and sensible thing to do is to get the expert to work out for you every detail of life, what is to be done and what is not to be done. That is what the scribes of the Pharisees did. They developed the Commandments into six hundred and eighteen commandments, positive and negative, and all of them designed to make it possible for honest and sincere men to do exactly what was required of them, and thereby to earn their place in the Kingdom of Heaven. It was exactly this which brought our Lord Jesus into conflict with the Pharisees, if only because there is a greater Law which no rules and regulations can embody. And further, as more than one psalmist knew right well, religion does not consist only in doing this or that, but even more, and indeed primarily, in being something. That something is being in a particular relationship with God. The Christian knows that from God's side it involves His redeeming love, and on his own side a humble, loving trust.

We turn to another matter, raised by Psalm 44.24,

> Why dost–thou–hide thy–face,
> Forgettest our–affliction and–our–oppression?

The idea of forgetting is one of the figures of speech adopted by the psalmist in order to express the 'delayed action' of God. Their problem, which recurs again and again, is the problem of the prosperity of the wicked and the misery of the righteous. They believe that in a God-ordered world, things ought to work the other way round, with prosperity to the righteous and misery for the wicked. Their

solution is that the doctrine of good fortune for the good
and bad fortune for the bad is quite sound, but that the
result is delayed. It is not for ever (9.18, Psalms 74, 75,
77); God is testing us (11.4f.); it is only for a moment
(30.5). Others say that God needs to awaken from sleep
(44.23 and 49.14 ' in the morning '); He must stir Himself up
(35.23) arise (82.8), and make haste (40.13 and 143.7). Or
again, perhaps God is hiding Himself (10.1), or He is far
away (22.1 and 19; 38.21). All of these phrases are attempts
to describe God's apparent absence from the place where the
psalmist is in his trouble. The expressions are anthropomorphic. It is not that anthropomorphic phrases as such
are to be avoided. They cannot be avoided, for in what
way are we to speak of God except in terms based on human
experience? The only alternative to this is to abstract all
ideas of personality from our thought of Him and our
expressions of those thoughts, unless perchance we are to
cease to speak of Him altogether. But these particular
phrases certainly do leave something to be desired. The
picture in 44.24 is one of forgetfulness. From this picture,
we get the idea of remembrance, this naturally being the
corresponding description of what happens when God
does at last take action. The clearest example is Psalm
9.12.

The statement that God ' remembers ' is found more than
once in the Old Testament. The outstanding cases in Jewish
tradition are God's remembrance of Rachel (Gen. 30.22),
to which is added the parallel case of Sarah, and God's
remembrance of Hannah (I Sam. 1.19). God's remembrance
therefore means that God is taking action. The idea of
remembrance took, and still does take a foremost place in
the ideas which are associated with the Jewish New Year
Festival. At this festival, in time past and still to this day,
amongst various other elements in the liturgy, a number of
passages of Scripture are recited by the Jews. These consist
of ten *Malkiyyoth*, passages which contain a reference to
Jehovah the King; ten *Zikronoth*, passages which contain

references to Jehovah remembering Israel; and ten *Shofaroth*, passages which contain references to the blowing of the *Shofar*, the ram's horn trumpet. The ten *Zikronoth* comprise three passages from the Law (Gen. 8.1; Ex. 2.24; Lev. 26.42); three passages from the Psalms (111.4; 111.5; 106.45); three passages from the Prophets (Jer. 2.2; Ezek. 16.60; Jer. 31.20), and they conclude with Leviticus 26.45. There is a liturgical manuscript of the Honan Jews of Kaifung-fu which has also a sixth passage from the Psalms, inserted between the fifth and sixth of these Remembrance verses, namely Psalm 105.8. The New Year is especially the time of God's remembering, because this is the time above all when the Jews looked forward, as we do now for our new year, to a change of fortune. But the important point is that for them remembrance did not mean 'take note of and file away for reference for future action'. It means remember and take action now. This use is similar to that of the verb 'hear' in Hebrew. It very often means more than 'hear', but 'hear and obey', and this is so especially in Deuteronomy and passages written under Deuteronomic influence.

When, therefore, the Jews spoke of a memorial, they meant a time when God took action. This is one way in which it is possible and legitimate to think of the Lord's Supper. When we say that it is a memorial, we can mean one of two things. We can mean that it is a memorial for us, in the sense that we remember Christ's death 'until He come'. We can mean also that it is a memorial for God. We cut out the anthropomorphism to the extent that we know He has no need to remember us because He has at any time forgotten us, but we keep that other element in the Jewish ideas. It means that it is a time when God takes action. And that is what the Lord's Supper is, whether we call it Lord's Supper, Holy Communion, Eucharist, and so forth. This is an occasion *par excellence* on which God is pleased to act. He can take action any time He pleases, and He is regularly taking 'saving' action on every kind of occasion, but here at this holy rite men and women have experienced this saving act of God more often and more readily than at any other times. This, then, is one way, and a more excellent way, of regarding the Lord's Supper as a memorial.

# IV

## Psalm 46

## CERTAINTY ABOUT GOD

THE THREE STANZA formation is very plain in this psalm. Also, we are all familiar with Martin Luther's *Ein feste Burg ist unser Gott*, and the firm, unshakable faith therein portrayed. Both psalm and hymn have been a consolation and an inspiration to generation after generation of believers.

The majority of commentators have associated this psalm and the two following psalms with the remarkable deliverance of Jerusalem in the time of Hezekiah from the army of Sennacherib. The story is found in II Kings 18.13—19.36 and again in Isaiah 36.1—37.38. Other identifications have been suggested, notably Jehoshaphat's victory over the Moabite-Edomite alliance (II Chron. 20), and even some unspecified deliverance at the end of the third century B.C. when the Ptolemies of Egypt and the Seleucids of Syria were struggling for the control of Palestine. Every identification must stop short of proof, and must be largely conjectural. There are rarely enough details in any psalms to warrant its positive identification with any specific historical event. The psalmist here certainly looks back with a great sense of thanksgiving on some great and unexpected deliverance in the immediate past. This is the basis of a tremendous confidence in God. God has evidently rescued the city when all hope had disappeared and when everything seemed to be lost.

God to–us (has been) shelter and–strength,
Help in–deep–distress he–has–been–found abundantly. (v. 1).

The most that can be said is that of all the incidents of
Hebrew history which are known to us, the deliverance
from the Assyrian Sennacherib is the most likely to have
been the occasion for such a psalm as this. Indeed the
whole matter of trust in God can best be discussed in relation to this particular historical event. It had a most remarkable influence on Hebrew thought. The extent of this
influence can partly be judged by the way in which it
received special and extensive attention in the eulogy of
Hezekiah which is to be found in Ecclesiasticus (Ben
Sirach) 48.17-25.

In his earlier years Hezekiah had followed the policy of
his father Ahaz and had remained a faithful vassal king
under Assyrian suzerainty. There is no evidence that the
Assyrians themselves occupied the country. Rather they
were content with regular tribute and homage. So little
interference was there that the Chronicler could ignore
altogether any suggestion of foreign domination, making
it appear that Sennacherib's punitive expedition of 701 B.C.
was the first contact with Assyria since Ahaz's appeal for
help in 734 B.C. (II Chron. 28.16 and 21; 32.1)—not that the
Chronicler really needed much encouragement, or even as
much justification as this, when he came to write the story
of this (to him) the most faithful of Judahite kings. As
C. C. Torrey and R. H. Pfeiffer have pointed out, the
Chronicler 'is a writer of great originality, vivid imagina-
tion and granite convictions'. But the accession of Sennacherib in 705 B.C. was the occasion of a general revolt
through the Assyrian Empire. Hezekiah himself joined
in the general revolt, allying himself with the subject kings
of the west, who all revolted, except three small Philistine
kings. Indeed, Hezekiah seems to have taken a leading
part in this western revolt, and he was uniformly successful
in the military expeditions which he undertook (II Kings

18.7-8). One of the Philistine kings who was faithful to Assyria was Padi of Ekron. He was driven out by his subjects, and Hezekiah imprisoned him in Jerusalem. The Judahite king overran all the loyal Philistine territory as far as Gaza, and all went well for some three or four years. By that time Sennacherib had put down the revolts in other parts of the empire and was able, though only for a short while, to turn his attention to the west. The revolt was soon crushed, and Hezekiah found himself shut up close in Jerusalem like a bird in a cage. He had to surrender his prisoner and pay a huge indemnity. It seems as though at first Sennacherib was content to reduce Hezekiah to immobility without occupying Jerusalem itself, but apparently he changed his mind and demanded full surrender. The accounts in the books of Kings are confused, and we have in fact three different accounts, which it is not easy to reconcile with each other in all details. It is certain that Jerusalem was besieged, and that the Assyrian high command appeared before the walls to point out the hopelessness and futility of further resistance.

But Jerusalem was not captured, neither did the city surrender. The besieging army suddenly disappeared, and according to II Kings 19.35, it was destroyed to the last man. The sudden change of front was remarkable, and Hezekiah and his men ascribed it to a direct intervention of the God of Israel. From the political point of view, Judah learned her lesson. She never again rebelled against the Assyrian kings, nor indeed against any overlord for a hundred years. Religiously, the effect of this deliverance was mixed. Judah gained a firmer faith in the saving power of God, but she forgot the conditions under which that saving power was exercised. In this she was in no way different from others, then or now. We, in our day, are as forgetful as our fathers have been. For us, the whole incident may be regarded both as an encouragement and as a warning.

Isaiah the prophet had always been against that reliance upon the promises of Egypt which had led Hezekiah and his friends into such serious trouble. He had spoken most violently against the embassy to Egypt (Isa. 30.1-5), and had steadily insisted that nothing but disaster, shame and confusion could come of it. Equally he had reproved Hezekiah for his friendly reception of Merodach-baladan of Babylon, that stormy petrel who had been responsible for the eastern section of the revolt (II Kings 20.12-20). Isaiah had proclaimed in the Name of the Holy One of Israel that Jerusalem's one hope of safety was a quiet confidence in God. Their salvation depended upon their turning back again to God in repentance and in a quiet neutrality (30.15). They must remain inactive so far as alliances were concerned, and must trust in God alone. When the king and his ministers refused to follow his advice, he promised rout and disaster. Helper and helped alike were both doomed to utter failure (31.3).

But when the last calamity of complete disaster and exile was hanging heavy with doom over the beleaguered city, Isaiah ceased to speak of disaster. When all was going well, he promised trouble and defeat. When things were at their worst, he promised rescue and salvation. According to II Kings 19.6 and 19.22-34, the turning point was the blasphemy of the Assyrian envoys. They jeered at Hezekiah and his last-ditch trust in his God (II Kings 18. 30). They shouted out with brutal insistence and vulgar words that the God of Israel was no more able to save His people than the gods of the other rebels had been able to save them from the might of Assyria (II Kings 18.33-35). The reply of the prophet was: ' I will defend this city to save it, for mine own sake, and for David my servant's sake' (19.34). The city was saved, though politically that was all that was saved, but a remnant of the house of Judah did escape to take root downward and to bear fruit upward (19.30). Isaiah's belief in the Remnant had led to a firm faith in God and His purposes.

The unexpected deliverance of the city and the temple proved to be a mixed blessing. On the credit side, it undoubtedly ensured the survival of both nation and religion. Judah learned her lesson, and henceforth steadily resisted every persuasion to rebel. The result was that when at last the Assyrians lost control at the death of Asshurbanipal in 626 B.C., there was still a native king in Jerusalem who could restore and reform the national worship. And this is what Josiah did, close after the removal of the Assyrian overlordship. In the north, repeated rebellion had robbed Israel of its own king, however subservient he might have had to be to his Assyrian master, with the result that, when deliverance came at last, there was no chance of reorganization and restoration. This was why Jeremiah fought so hard in his day for the same policy of quiet inactivity in the face of the Babylonian supremacy a hundred years later. Humanly speaking, therefore, we and all the human race owe everything to Isaiah's steadfast trust in this time of disaster.

Isaiah had been insistent enough in his earlier years, and indeed close up to the time of crisis, upon the absolute necessity of true loyalty to God and right action between man and man. In common with the other eighth century B.C. prophets, he had been combating the general belief that God was bound to rescue Israel from all her troubles solely, in the last resort, because He was Israel's God and Israel was His people. The prophets rightly insisted that this was not enough. It might be satisfactory for the Moabites to think in this way about Chemosh and his people Moab, or for the Ammonites to think so about Milcom and his people Ammon, but it was not enough for Israel. Jehovah is a God of righteousness and He demands righteousness from His people Israel. Not even regular and persistent sacrifices were enough, however sedulously maintained and scrupulously observed. These must be backed up by true living. God demands from His people that they do what is right, keep the covenant and be humble before Him. God will have nothing to do with extortioners, murderers and adulterers, however faithfully they trample His courts. 'Cease to do evil; seek true justice, set right the oppressed, plead the widow's cause' (Isa. 1.16-17). If Israel is willing to listen and to obey in these matters, then Israel will prosper. There is no future otherwise for Jehovah's people, however much it be true that Israel is Jehovah's. The prophet's message, therefore, during his earlier years consisted of condemnation, relieved by impassioned pleas for repentance and hope for a surviving, faithful and repentant remnant.

The hope of a faithful remnant appears in three distinct forms. First, there is the plain expectation that there will be a small company, however woefully small, who will repent and turn back to God again (1.27), those that will remain after all the filth has been washed away (4.3-4). Second, there is the expectation that a prince of the royal house will be born, and that there will be no limit to the steady increase of his territory and the national prosperity (9.7), and in his days and for ever thereafter there will be an endless halcyon peace (11.1-9). Third, there is this last expectation that Jerusalem will be saved, though as a brand snatched from the burning. Ultimately, therefore, however much Isaiah is convinced of his people's waywardness and sin, he cannot bring himself in the last resort to think of their complete extinction.

It may be that Isaiah's certainty of Jerusalem's salvation even in the throes of final disaster was due, at least in part, to his own human and patriotic sentiments. We all tend to be influenced in this way. It is noteworthy that every prophet tends to be more sure of judgment and punishment when he is speaking about the other section of the People of God. Equally every prophet is more sure of mercy and forbearance when he is speaking about his own section. Amos the southerner has no hope at all for the northern kingdom. Similarly Isaiah himself regards the destruction of the northern kingdom as certain (28). He too was a southerner. Hosea knows that disaster is inevitable for Israel, but he hopes with fervent zeal for a restoration and a new beginning. He was a northerner. Isaiah has hope for Judah, though only of a remnant. Jeremiah, speaking after Israel had ceased to exist, and knowing that surrender was all that was left for Judah, looks forward to a time when both Israel and Judah will find new life in a common union. Jeremiah was descended from that Abiathar who was exiled by Solomon to Ananoth, and Abiathar is generally accepted as being sole survivor of the massacred Shiloh priesthood, the ancient priesthood of the Ark from the earliest days. The family had lived in the south for four hundred years, so that Jeremiah had deep affection for both north and south. It may be, therefore, that Isaiah was influenced by his own love for his own people, and especially by his veneration for the Temple in which he had received his original call to be a prophet. Perhaps, like his immediate predecessor Hosea, he knew enough of human love and devotion to realize something of the tension and agony portrayed in Hosea 11.1-11. In any case, it is certain that there is a love which cannot let Israel go, a God whose forbearance far outpasses all human limits, to whom the seventy-times-seven is no extraordinary feat of forgiveness, but normal, steady and continuous. But there is a limit even to the forbearance of God, as Mark 12.1-9 makes clear. 'He had yet one son, a beloved son; he sent him last unto them, saying, They will reverence my son . . . And they took him and killed him . . . What therefore will the lord of the vineyard do? He will come and destroy the husband-men.'

The danger of Israel's conviction that city and temple would not be destroyed was that the people might think that God was bound to save Jerusalem always, just because the temple was there. Something of this is evident in Psalm 46.5 :

God (is) in–the–midst–of–her; she–shall–not–be–moved; God shall–help–her at–the–turn–of the–morning.

The belief in the inviolability of Zion because of the

presence there of the Temple did indeed bear evil fruit, and it was one of the factors which made Jeremiah's task so difficult a century later. 'Trust ye not in lying words, saying, The Temple of the Lord, the Temple of the Lord are these' (Jer. 7.4). He continued to reiterate what Isaiah himself would certainly have said, that injustice and apostasy on the part of the worshippers necessarily involved the destruction of the Temple. The Temple itself was as much a haunt of wickedness as any other place. It was false and useless to say, having neglected in every way to do God's will, 'We are sure to be delivered,' and then to make use of God's forbearance to continue with every sort of abomination. They may call it God's house twice over, and three times over for that matter, but it is nothing but a den of robbers. What happened to Shiloh will surely happen to Jerusalem, and for the very same reason. Thus the wheel turned full circle. Their fathers had falsely held that God must save them whatever they did. Now they said that God must save the Temple whatever they did. In the olden days any advance in religious ideas was prevented by such false ideas. Now retrogression was certain, and this must always be the case whenever men substitute anything else for full trust in God and that godly living which follows therefrom.

John Bunyan was right when he wrote that the pilgrim's path is beset with every kind of peril from the moment he leaves the City of Destruction even to the midst of the river which laps the walls of the Celestial City. And Ignorance even got as far as the Gate. 'There was a way to Hell, even from the Gate of Heaven, as well as from the City of Destruction.' Those very things which most can help along the heavenly road can be the very things which lead men astray. This is because men in every generation will substitute anything and everything for the basic necessity of faith. In fact the truer the aid, the falser it may prove. The Temple itself was the most important of all the visible means by which a man might find himself in the presence of the living God, but the Temple itself became Israel's greatest snare. This happened twice, and twice the Temple was destroyed. Men trusted in the Temple, and forgot that the very Temple itself was but a means to an end. The climax in the life of Jesus was when He repeated these words of Jeremiah's concerning the den of robbers. It was then that the priests joined with the Pharisees and the Herodians to destroy Him. It was the words of Jesus against the Temple that sealed His doom.

This same thing can happen in respect of ritual observances when men come to trust in them and in the precise performance of them. It can happen also when men reject these observances, and trust in their emancipation from them and their perils. On the one side there is the Scylla of liturgies and rituals which have become an end in themselves; on the other side there is the Charybdis of that spiritual pride which can arise out of self-congratulation at being safe from the snares in which we see others to be entangled. The same is true of all kinds of religious activities. It is possible to be so fully engrossed in good works that these become an end in themselves and the true goal is forgotten. One thing alone is essential, and nothing must be permitted to lead us astray from it. This one thing is a firm and full trust and reliance upon God, out of which there must proceed 'all such good works as God has prepared for us to walk in'.

This firm faith the psalmist undoubtedly had, a faith firm enough to endure though the very earth be changed. It would be true to say that this man's faith was not shaken by disaster, but that on the contrary it was strengthened by it. If this man could have such a faith as this without any hope of any life beyond the grave, how much more sure should be the faith of the Christian when he has the hope of immortality! This psalmist was not like the writer of Psalm 37, who wilfully shut his eyes to the facts (37.25), and roundly declared that never in all his long life had he ever seen the righteous forsaken or his seed begging for bread.

Our psalmist knew the facts, faced them, and was all the more certain of his faith. His head remained 'bloody but unbowed'. Why? What was the nature and ground of this cast-iron certainty? Let us turn to another scene altogether, the scene in which Jesus faces His last days on earth. Here was One also who knew better than to accept the facts which He could see, and He would have us also look beyond the events themselves, lest we fail to realize just what is the shadow and what is the reality.

Imagine a traveller arriving in Jerusalem on that first Palm Sunday. He would have found the main street thronged with a tumultuous crowd, running, cheering, waving branches of trees, olives and palms. In the midst of the crowd, riding along quietly on a young ass-colt was Jesus of Nazareth, hailed by the whole crowd as the long-expected Messiah, entering at last the city of his father David. Everywhere he looked this visitor would have seen men wildly enthusiastic for the rider of the ass, and he would have had to search with the utmost determination for any who were not joining in the general jubilation. He would have said, and would have had no slightest doubt but that he was right, that this was victory for Jesus of Nazareth and defeat for those that hated Him. But supposing that this traveller had arrived on the following Friday instead, he would have found the huge crowd outside the city, watching a triple execution. He would have seen three crosses with Jesus of Nazareth hanging on the middle one. He would have seen jeering, exulting groups everywhere, or men indifferently passing by. He might possibly have noticed a small group who were overwhelmed with sorrow, but once again he would have had to search determinedly. And he would have said, and he would have had no slightest doubt but that he was right, that this was defeat for Jesus of Nazareth and victory for those that hated Him. Never has there been a defeat apparently so ignominious and complete; but as it has turned out these nineteen hundred years, never has there been an incident which has proved to be less a defeat, and now the Name of Jesus is revered in countless lands where even the eagles of the Caesars never flew.

It is certain that both Jewish priest and Roman procurator thought that they had made an end of this Jesus of Nazareth with His strange compelling power, and for some seven weeks or so, it looked as if they had been right. There were odd rumours of His having appeared to those who knew Him best and loved Him most, and there was some mysterious talk about the disappearance of the Body. But at the Feast of Pentecost the whole affair flared up again, with a hundred and twenty men and women rushing down the stairs headlong into the street declaring with the utmost conviction that God had raised Jesus from the dead, and had bestowed upon them that supernatural power of which the prophet Joel had spoken. Three thousand men forthwith declared their adherence to this inspired company. Quickly the movement spread throughout Judea, until the authorities realized that it was high time to stamp out this fire that had been kindled. They were too late, and in any case they scattered the fire only to see it spring up again with new vigour, here, there and everywhere. The time came when the group was joined by one of its most talented and zealous enemies, the young Saul, a rabbi born in Tarsus of Cilicia but now domiciled in Jerusalem. This Saul became Paul the Apostle of the Gentiles, and he spread the good news far and wide through the eastern half of the Roman Empire. He and his fellows endured extreme hardships, perils of every kind, all the dangers which beset the traveller by land and sea at a time when they had not even the partial control of wind and weather that we have to-day, a time when neither roads nor seas were safe. They showed great endurance in every kind of tribulation— imprisonment, riots, floggings, hunger and thirst, 'dying and behold we live, chastened but not killed', 'bearing branded on the body the marks of Jesus'.

This persistent endeavour, pursued with utter self-abandonment, has been the characteristic of the apostles of Christ in every generation. Again and again apparent defeat has been changed into demonstrable victory. The reason for this is that the real battlefield is not outside where men can see, in busy city streets and the crowded market-places of the world. The real battlefield is inside in the hearts of men, inside where none can see. This is the only place where victory can be achieved or defeat registered. Whoever loses there, can never win; whoever is conqueror there must conquer everywhere. The apostles of Christ have been unconquerable because of the victory that has been achieved in their own hearts.

It would be foolish to maintain that none but Christians are stout-hearted, and that only *they* have, by determined steadfastness, been able to snatch victory out of defeat. The history of the world is full of such inspiring stories: Thotmes III of Egypt rescuing his scattered column from the charging Hittites in North Syria in the fifteenth century B.C.; the Spartans at Thermopylae and the Athenians at Marathon and Salamis; the persistence of Rome against Pyrrhus of Epirus for six long years in the earlier part of the third century B.C. or again against Hannibal towards the end of that same century, when he maintained himself for fifteen years in Italy and Sicily before Carthagian troubles elsewhere recalled him; and so endlessly, coming down into British history, such battles as Albuera and all the way down to Dunkirk. 'We went to the fight and we fell; but we still go, and we still will go, whenever it is required of us.' Peace, too, has its stories of the defeated who refused to know defeat, in the early days of the reform movements, farm labourers, cotton weavers, lords and peasants, all through our grades of society, for no class has a monopoly of devotion, though usually the poor have had more need of it than the rich. Bad causes have had their martyrs as well as good causes, from Mattan onwards, that high priest of Baal who died rather than desert the altar of his false god (II Kings 11.18). There is nothing more praiseworthy just as often as there has been nothing more tragic, than the devoted constancy with which a man will sacrifice everything for the cause which he has enthroned in his heart.

Is there any difference, then, between the certainty of the religious man and any other kind of certainty? The answer is that there are two kinds of certainty. There is the certainty which depends upon logical argument. It is an intellectual certainty. There is also the certainty which arises out of personal relationships. The first is the kind of certainty which is shown at its clearest in mathematics. Consider, for example, a simple quadratic equation:

$$x^2 - 4x + 4 = 0$$
$$(x - 2)^2 = 0$$
$$x = 2$$

There can be no doubt whatever about this. Given the premise, the conclusion is certain. This is the kind of certainty which belongs particularly to abstract problems where the data are known. The difficulty about most so-called scientific certainties is that we can never be sure that we know all the data. All that certainty in scientific matters means is that, assuming that we have all the data, then this conclusion is certain. It follows that in matters scientific there must always be a measure of uncertainty, and no reputable man of science will ever claim anything but a varying degree of probability. But, where the data are fully known, there we can have absolute intellectual certainty. But there is another kind of certainty, that which springs out of relationships between persons. The best example is that of a couple who fall in love with each other. They are quite certain about each other, and the more certain they are, the less they are prepared to listen to what anybody else may say. But there is no question of the certainty. But when this couple has lived together over a number of years, there arises a certainty that is deeper and sounder than any at first. It is built on years of mutual trust and knowledge, and it is to be seen in the successful marriages of the middle-aged. Further, when it comes to the last resort, men and women will act on the basis of this type of certainty against, if need be, the kind of certainty that comes by intellectual apprehension. This is why men and women will sometimes do things which to everybody else are rankly stupid and unreasonable, because of the love they bear to each other. This type of action in a time of crisis is paramount. It showed itself in all sorts of heroic actions which were done during the war in times of peril and danger. Men and women did unreasonable things, things which cold logic would condemn out of hand, and they did them because of this other kind of certainty which, in times of crisis, will put persons first and syllogisms and the rest second. This is the type of certainty which I, for one, have about God. It is not contrary to reason, and given its own premises it is as logical as the rest. But it has its own premises, and they are the premises which have their basis in personal experience of a Person. Nobody ever argued me into it, and I am quite certain that nobody can ever argue me out of it. It never depended on that type of argument. If anyone should ask me how it is that I am sure of God, I could give no answer except that it is in the same kind of way in which I am sure of my wife. Just how it is that I am sure of that, I do not know. It has been strengthened by the intimacies and mutual trust of the years, but it began . . . ? The Christian is prepared to give reasons for the faith that is in him, but his faith does not depend upon such reasons. The soundest example in the Bible is Jeremiah.

This man, Jeremiah, is an outstanding example of a man whose whole life and action were determined by the conviction and certainty which were grounded in his personal relation with God. He is the prophet above all others who seems to have been called to do things and to say things which were contrary to his own nature. His work as a prophet was never simple and straightforward, as, for instance, was the case with Amos. Amos's message was wholly in accord with all his earlier training and with all we can detect about his character. Jeremiah was true to his name—*Jahu hurls, Jahu throws*, for it is God and not Jeremiah who determines the course of Jeremiah's life, and this all the more clearly because so very often the course is directly opposite to that which Jeremiah's own inclinations would suggest. And yet, in spite of this tension between his own disposition and the course of action which was laid upon him, there is no man who shows more clearly how great and dominating can be the inner certainty which comes from communion with God. Jeremiah was a man who naturally depended much on ordinary companionship. There are some men who can stand alone, who delight to stand alone, and seem happiest when they are in a minority which consists of one. Not so Jeremiah, for as soon as he came up against opposition, he withdrew into himself as though to wonder in his own heart whether or not he was right. He was greatly troubled by opposition, and speaks in Jeremiah 20.7-10 of the considerable perturbation of soul which was his in the face of opposition. Again, there are many passages in his oracles which show him to be the kind of man who would be the ideal husband and father, but he found himself sure that he was called of God to be neither. Yet again, no man was more patriotic than Jeremiah, but he found himself driven to proclaim a message which involved nothing short of surrender for his country. His mission as a prophet seems to be so much at variance with his natural desires that Hans Wildberger[1] has based his psychological study of the phenomena of prophecy on the life and work of Jeremiah, on the ground that where there is such an apparent contradiction it is easiest to discern what difference the prophetic inspiration can make. This Jeremiah made two early essays in prophecy, and each time he was wrong. He prophesied on the advent of the Scythian invasion that Jerusalem would fall

[1] *Jahwewort und prophetische Rede bei Jeremia*, Zurich, 1942.

(1.13-19), and then later he supported the Deuteronomic reforms (11.1-5) only to find that, as things worked out (8.8) he was once more on the wrong side. Each time he had spoken from inner conviction, and had said, 'Thus saith the Lord,' only to find that his message was wrong. And so we get a silence. He said that he would speak no more in Jehovah's name (20.9), only to find that there was in his heart as it were a burning fire shut up in his bones, so that at last he could no longer contain himself. Henceforth he was right, and it was truly 'Thus saith the Lord'. The explanation is that this man, longing for companionship and bereft of all human companionship, with even his own people trying to murder him, was driven to seek fellowship with God in a way that no man previously had found it. He, first of men, came to know that inner certainty of conviction which is based on true fellowship with God. This is the root and basis of the certainty of the Christian, and no man can truly speak of Christianity without it.

# V

*Psalm 50*

## THE HIGH GOD SPEAKS

THIS PSALM is the 'lonely' Asaphite psalm, separated
from its fellows by a whole block of Davidic psalms. As
we have pointed out in the first chapter, the probability is
that the original order was 2-41, 51-72, 42-49, 50, 73-83, an
arrangement which brings all the Davidic psalms together
at the beginning, then all the Sons of Qorach psalms, and
lastly all twelve Asaphite psalms. The psalm is in three
clear sections. The first section (1-6) describes Jehovah, the
High God, summoning all the earth to hear His declared
will. The second section (7-15) contains His message to
faithful Israel; God requires neither sheep nor goats,
whether wholly offered upon the altar or mostly eaten by
the worshippers at the great sacred pilgrimage feasts. He
demands true thank-offerings and the sincere fulfilment of
vows. The third section (16-22) is God's Word to the
wicked, the men who talk about His Law, pay Him lip
service, but by their conduct give the lie to every word
they say. The psalm closes with a renewed demand for
thank-offerings, and a declaration that this is the way of
salvation.

The psalm opens:

Jehovah (is) the–Chief–of the–gods.
He–hath–spoken and–hath–summoned–the–earth,
From–the–rising–of–the–sun to–its–setting. (v. 1).

The verse declares that Jehovah is the chief of the gods. He is El, the High God. This is the name of the head of the Canaanite pantheon. In the recently discovered Ugarit texts, all the deities prostrate themselves before El, and seek his permission whatever it is they design to do. Usually the Virgin Anat, Queen of Heaven, Mother of the gods, intercedes on their behalf. It is not easy to decide whether this psalmist is a strict monotheist, believing that Jehovah is the only God, or whether he is a henotheist, worshipping one God only, but not denying the existence of other gods. If the phrase 'El of the gods' is to be taken literally, then the psalmist is certainly not a monotheist. But it cannot be said for certain that this is the case. It may very well be, and indeed is more likely than not, that the phrase 'El of the gods' is an ancient survival which has lived on into a truly monotheistic period. Religious phraseology, liturgy and ritual are full of ancient phrases and customs which have persisted from less developed times. We still speak of the Anger of God. The phrase undoubtedly goes back to a time when men believed that God could be angry as men are angry, and used to flare out in sudden anger at men just as men sometimes flare out angrily at each other. The outstanding example of such action being ascribed to God is the story of the fate of Uzzah (II Sam. 6.7). David was bringing the Ark up to Jerusalem to the accompaniment of tremendous excitement and a very great deal of noise from various instruments, all of them particularly calculated to rouse unrestrained emotion, after the general Eastern style. It is not surprising that the oxen became restive and started to bolt. Whereupon Uzzah automatically and un-thinkingly put out his hand to steady the Ark, which doubt-less was rocking dangerously on its somewhat primitive carriage. 'And the anger of the Lord was kindled against Uzzah, and God smote him there.' The modern, and more correct explanation of the incident is that as soon as Uzzah touched the Ark, he realized that he had touched a forbid-den object. He had broken a *tabu* of the utmost awesomeness, and the shock of it had killed him on the spot. There are many instances of this kind of thing happening amongst peoples where religious ideas are of the primitive *mana*-type. The phrase 'Anger of God' still survives, but, for the Christian, it is not a non-rational, nor even a semi-rational reaction on the part of God. We preserve the phrase to express God's steady antagonism to sin. This is not by any means a sudden, impatient reaction, but a steady, purposeful hostility. Another result of this idea of 'holy' things which must not be approached by the ordinary man involved the shutting-off of the Holy Place from persons who were not consecrated. This custom still survives in churches of some communions, though the original primitive ideas have been wholly transformed.

Or again, it is the custom, almost universal, for Anglican churches to be built so that the centre line of the nave runs on the east-west line. There is not the slightest doubt but that the original significance of this is associated with the worship of the rising sun, and that the altar was placed in such a position that the beams of the rising sun fell directly on it at the proper season of the year (cf. Stonehenge). With the comparatively recent custom whereby the altar is placed at the east end of the building, this ancient custom has become altogether obscured. In the olden days, the custom was for all to turn towards the rising sun at the proper occasion during the ritual. With the placing of the altar at the east end, this custom has been changed into turning towards the altar. But no one who worships regularly, or for that matter irregularly, in a church of this type ever thinks that he is turning towards the rising sun. When he turns towards the east, if he be priest or chorister, he is following the age-old pagan custom, but a new reason has supplanted the original. The direction is now said to be eastwards because that is the direction in which Jerusalem lies for Christians of the west; or, since Archbishop Laud moved the altar to the east end, because the worshipper believes that in some special sense God Himself is present there.

There is another case of an ancient survival in verse 1 of the psalm, though this is geographical and astronomical rather than religious. The English Versions have 'unto the going down thereof', i.e. unto the going down of the sun at evening time. The Hebrew has 'to his entrance'. It is a relic of the days when the sun-god 'went out' in the dawn from his bed-chamber, and 'entered' it again at sunset. This idea of 'going out' appears in Isaiah 40.26, where we read 'that bringeth out their host by number . . .' The meaning is that it is God who makes all the stars rise at the proper time, one after the other, and not one of them rises out of turn or does not rise at all.

The second verse of the psalm reads:

> From—Zion, perfection—of—beauty,
> God hath—shone—forth—glitteringly.  (v. 2).

Here we have a transformation from the old Ugarit mythology. Far away in the North (Zaphon) is the great mountain of the North. The road hither is flanked by two great mountains. These are called 'the flanks (sides) of the North' (cf. Isa. 14.13; Ezek. 38.6 and 15; 39.2, and especially Psalm 48.1f.). In Psalm 48 the ancient phrases have been preserved, and they have been transferred to Mount Zion. This has happened to a minor extent in the phrase 'perfection of beauty', which originally was a reference to the mountain of the North. The shrines of Palestine were invariably on hill-tops, and for this reason they were called high-places. The reason for their position on the hill-tops was not because thus they were nearest to the sky, nor was it (as some say concerning English parish churches) because thus they were free from flooding, though this certainly has something to do with it in the Fen country. The reason is that they were replicas of the great Mount of God away in the far North. It is impossible for mortal man to reach that far-off divine abode, because of all the perils of that mystic way. But the god, in his goodness and mercy, encourages men to build a model of his great place on the holy mountain, in order that men may ascend this holy hill and find God there. The earthly shrine on the local hill-top is thus a model, a replica, a symbolical copy of the god's true home. At Jerusalem there were two bronze pillars, separate from the main building but close in front of the entrance porch. More than one explanation has been proposed for the presence of these two bronze pillars which Hiram cast and set up for king Solomon. The most likely suggestion is that they represent the twin mountains which flanked the road to the mount of the North. The worshippers passed between Jachim and Boaz (I Kings 7.15 and 21), and thus symbolically they passed between those mysterious twin mountains which flank the road to the Palace of God.

There is another survival to be found in Psalm 46.4, 'There is a river, whose streams make glad the city of God.' The commentators have had very great difficulty here in their attempts to identify this river with an actual river. There is no river anywhere near Jerusalem which can be called a *nahar*. It is best to adopt the suggestion which sees here a reference to the ancient sacred river of eastern lore. It appears in Samuel Taylor Coleridge's fragment entitled *Kubla Khan*—

> Where Alph, the sacred river, ran
> Through caverns measureless to man
> Down to a sunless sea.

It is part of the ancient myth of the Garden of God. It was on the top of a mountain, surrounded by impenetrable thickets. The Hebrews called this garden 'Eden', and in Ezekiel 28.14 it is described as being upon 'the holy mountain of God'. Milton has retained this in his description of Paradise, and he has also retained the legend of the overgrown thicket:

So on he fares, and to the border comes
Of Eden, where delicious Paradise,
Now nearer, crowns with her enclosure green,
As with a rural mound, the champain head
Of a steep wilderness, whose hairy sides
With thicket overgrown, grotesque and wild,
Access denied.

(PARADISE LOST, Book iv, lines 130-137).

He continues by describing all the numerous trees which
grew in this garden, Ezekiel 31.9. The garden contained
jewelled trees (cf. Ezek. 28.13), and it is eight hundred
years since the great Jewish commentator, Rashi, saw in
Ezekiel 28.14 ('in the midst of the stones of fire') a reference to the jewelled trees of Paradise. There is a relic of
this in the Grimms' fairy tale of the twelve princesses. In
this Garden of God there was a river, which split into four
streams. To the Hebrews these were the four great rivers
of the ancient world (Gen. 2.10-14). The account in Genesis
2.4b-4.26 has come down through a desert medium. But
this fabled river of Paradise took its place in Hebrew lore,
and appears as the miraculous river of Ezekiel 47.1-12,
which flows out in the prophet's vision from the glorious
restored Temple. It swelled amazingly so that within a
distance of less than a mile (three thousand cubits is less
than a mile) it was too deep to be forded. This river (verse
7) had numerous trees on both sides of it. The image is
caught up again in Revelation 22.1-2, where it is the River
of Life. The river ran down the midst of the street of the
Holy City, but instead of many trees, we have the one tree,
the Tree of Life, strangely growing on both sides of the
river. There is probably a reference to this same mystic
river in Psalm 36.8, 'Thou shalt make them drink of
the river of thy pleasures,' and again in Psalm 65.9.

The psalmist represents God as bursting forth in splendour, shining forth with glittering light. This verb is frequently found in descriptions of the Splendour of God (Deut.

33.2 and Psalms 80.1; 94.1; Job 10.3). There are two traditions concerning Jehovah and His abode. One is that He
dwells in thick, impenetrable darkness, but the other is that
He is surrounded by blinding light. The two ideas appear
together in Deuteronomy 4.11, in the description there of
the theophany of Sinai: 'And the mountain burned with
fire unto the heart of heaven, with darkness, cloud and
thick darkness.' Similarly in Deuteronomy 5.23. The two
traditions appear also in Exodus 14.20, where the writer tells
of the way in which God Himself came between the fleeing
Israelites and the pursuing Egyptians. This was in the pillar
of cloud (14.19). The writer says, 'and there was the cloud
and the darkness, yet it gave light by night.' This passage
belongs to the J-tradition. Later, in the P-tradition, it is
described (Ex. 14.24) as a pillar of fire and cloud.

The inner shrine of Solomon's Temple was a window-
less room, completely dark (I Kings 8.12f.). We read:
'Then spake Solomon, Jehovah hath said that he would
dwell in thick darkness. I have surely built thee a house of
habitation, a place for thee to dwell for ever.' It is probable
that the origin of both the darkness and the brightness is
the violent summer thunderstorms of a semi-tropical country,
the type of storm which seems to be becoming more frequent
in Britain during recent years. The sky becomes very dark
indeed, and then, out of what sometimes can almost approxi-
mate to pitch darkness, there come the most brilliant continuous flashes of lightning. In such a storm there is an eeriness
which even the most sophisticated feel, and it is easy to see
how such a storm could have become the basis of the regular
figure for the advent of God. Both the excessive darkness
and the excessive brightness have their interpretations, the
one standing for the mystery of Deity and the other for the
splendour of His irresistible power.

Such sudden storms are usually accompanied with a sudden deluge of rain which turns the smallest of creeks into
a raging torrent, so that everything is swept away by it, men,
cattle, frame-houses, everything. In Texas they call it a

flash-flood. This is the meaning of the Hebrew *sheṭeph* (cf.
Isa. 28.15), and anyone who has once seen one of these
extraordinary storms and its consequences can have no
shadow of doubt of the meaning of such a passage. The
root is used frequently in the Old Testament, quite often
of the flooding downpour (so exactly in Ezek. 13.11 and 13;
38.22) of Jehovah's judgment.

The brightness with which God shines forth resplendently
became more and more a recognized metaphor for the
Presence of God. When Moses came down from Mount
Sinai with the two tables of testimony in his hands, the skin
of his face sent out rays of light (lit. 'horned') because he
had been speaking with God, so much so that Moses (so
says the P-tradition, Ex. 34.30) had to wear a veil over his
face. Moses, according to the tradition is the only man
'whom the Lord knew face to face' (Deut. 34.10). This
luminous cloud becomes the sign of the Presence of God.
This is the way in which the writer of Kings describes
Jehovah taking up His abode in the Temple which Solomon
had built. 'And it came to pass, when the priests came
out of the holy place, that the cloud filled the house of the
Lord, so that the priests could not stand to minister by
reason of the cloud: for the glory of the Lord filled the house
of the Lord' (I Kings 8.10-11). It is the *Shekinah* (i.e.
Presence) of New Testament times. It may very well be
that this was in the thought of the author of John 1.14:
'And the Word was made flesh and *dwelt* (the Greek word
is *eskenosen*) among us.' The choice of the Greek word is
probably not due to the idea of 'tabernacling among us',
as many suppose, but to the assonance which exists between
the Greek word 'to dwell in a tent' and the Hebrew word
*Shekinah*, which means 'dwelling-place'. This is all the
more likely because the verse goes on to say 'and we beheld
his *glory* (cf. I Kings 8.11 and many other cases), glory as
of the only begotten of the Father', and the whole context
concerns the true Light. Or again, there is the luminous
cloud of the Transfiguration (Mark 9.2). They had gone

up into a high mountain. Here once again we have a mountain as a sacred place, and this is a high mountain. His garment became glistening white (verse 3), and ' there came a cloud overshadowing them: and there came a voice out of the cloud '. Yet again, at the Ascension (Acts 1.9), the description is that ' he was taken up, and a cloud received him out of their sight '. This was not any odd cloud that happened to be there, for such a cloud is not characteristic of the Palestinian skyscape. The writer is referring to the Cloud of the Presence of God.

(Our–God shall–come, and–let–him–not–be silent)
Fire–before–him devours,
And–round–about–him (there is a) mighty shuddering.

(v. 3).

The first line has been bracketed because it is probably a later insertion. It is customary to assume that the Hebrew word *nis'arah* (shuddering) has to do with the intensity and violence of the storm-wind, but it is better to understand it in the sense 'bristle with horror', as in Ezekiel 27.35 and 32.10, and probably also Deuteronomy 32.17. Here once again we have the *mysterium tremendum* of which Rudolf Otto wrote in his *The Idea of the Holy,* that shuddering awe which betokens the presence of deity. We may compare Genesis 15.12 (which is JE), with its reference to the ' horror of darkness ' which fell upon Abraham before God passes between the pieces of the carcases in the image of a smoking fire-pot, and so ratifies His covenant with Abraham after the traditional fashion, common in more ancient countries than one. This primitive idea of awe is, as we have seen, at first non-ethical in character, but in the course of time it has come to have a predominantly ethical content. It is a mistake to follow the fashion of modern sentimental thinkers who would interpret this awe as the fear with which the wicked are seized. There is an awe and a consequent humbleness of spirit before God which it is well that all men should recognize. There can never be any question of equality between God and man. When all is said and done, God is always Creator and man the creature.

> He—calls to—the—heavens above,
> And—to—the—earth to—judge his—people.  (v. 4).

It is not necessary for us to assume that we have here a picture of the Final Judgment, nor is it necessary to see in the couplet a cultic coronation ceremony with the new king giving his decrees. The judgment which God is about to give is the declaration of His sovereign will, His decisions and the statement of what He requires from men. The use of the word *din* (judge) is similar to that in Zechariah 3.7, where Joshua the high priest is commissioned to govern the Lord's house.

> Gather—me my—faithful—ones,
> Those—who—keep my—covenant concerning—sacrifice.
>                                                      (v. 5).

The phrase 'my faithful ones' stands for the Hebrew word *chasid*, and here, beyond question, the word is connected with the idea of the covenant, as the second line of the couplet plainly shows. We have discussed this word *chasid* and the corresponding word *chesed* in connection with Psalm 42-43. The word *chasid* describes the faithful in Israel who have maintained the covenant and have sought earnestly to fulfil its every detail. In the Old Testament the word *chesed* when it is used to describe God's attitude to men is necessarily confined to His attitude to those who are within the covenant. It stands, therefore, for God's supremest benevolence to the privileged few. It does not stand for a general benevolence which flows everywhere and anywhere. It speaks of a loving, saving energy which is canalized. The essential significance of the New Testament word *charis* (grace) arises out of the idea of this special favour to a limited group. Paul's zeal for the conversion of the Gentiles was not due to general humanitarian notions, but to his belief that in Christ the middle wall of partition was broken down, so that God's special favour was fully and freely available for all mankind. It did not arise out of the notion of a general kindness wide as creation, but out of the idea of a special and particular favour which had fanned out. This difference is between a broad river spreading lazily into a wide plain, and, by contrast, a river held back by a dam and then released through a narrow culvert, with all the extra power engendered by the previous holding, confining power of the dam. This is one instance where the interpretation of a New Testament word as though it is a classical Greek word can lead to serious error. The word *charis* does not mean general kindness to all and sundry—just this and nothing more. It does indeed carry this much of its classical and Septuagint meaning, but its main motif is from the Hebrew *chesed*, the determined faithfulness of the covenant-love of God towards His covenant-people. It includes the element of undeservedness on the part of the recipient which can be included in the classical *charis*, but it preserves also a sacrificing love which far outstrips all human imaginings, born of a unique and divinely-originated relationship.

The last line of the couplet in verse 5 is not easy of interpretation. It is the custom to interpret the line as meaning 'make a covenant with sacrifice', the emphasis being laid (ever since Robertson Smith's time) on the fact that the Hebrew word *zebach* (the word used here for 'sacrifice') was strictly used of that type of offering of which by far the larger part was eaten by the worshippers. Professor Robertson Smith was a great advocate of the totemistic theory of the origin of religion with its dominant emphasis on the note that the totem-god and the totem-pole were one group. He was therefore strongly in favour of the idea that in the *zebach* we have a ceremonial feast in which the god and the people shared a common meal, and thus the union between god and people was restored and strengthened. Thus 'those that make my covenant by *zebach*' would refer to those who share in this common meal during the celebrations especially of the great pilgrimage feasts of Israel, Unleavened Bread, Weeks, and Ingathering, but chiefly the last, which was the greatest of the three, the one which marked the end of one year and the beginning of the next. But the more natural translation of the Hebrew here is 'concerning sacrifice', and in view of the fact that section two of the psalm (verses 8-14) speaks against another type of sacrifice, it is extremely probable that here the psalmist is speaking definitely in favour of the *zebach* type, just as later he seems to be speaking wholly against the '*olah* (whole offering) type.

In verse 8, we get the contrast between these two types, the *zebach*, which was mostly eaten by the worshippers, only a small portion going to the altar, and the '*olah* (the whole burnt offering), which was wholly consumed on the altar. God's declaration to faithful Israel is:

Not concerning–your–*zebachs* do–I–reprove–you;
(but) your–'*olahs* are–continually right–in–front–of–me.

(v. 8).

We have translated the Hebrew copula as 'but' (as is legitimate whenever a contrast is implied), because the next verses make it quite plain that God does not require this type of sacrifice.

I–will–not–take from–your–house a–bullock,
From–your–folds he-goats.
For–mine (is) every–wild–beast–of the–bad–lands,
The–cattle on–a–thousand–hills.
I–know every–bird of–the–heavens,[1]
And–the–live–creatures of–the–countryside are–in–my–
care.

[1] So the ancient versions.

If–I–were–hungry, I–would–not–tell you,
For–mine (is) the–world and–its–fulness.
Shall–I–eat the–flesh–of strong–beasts,
And–drink the–blood–of he-goats? (vv. 9-13).

On the basis of these verses, some writers have maintained that this psalmist is against the whole of the sacrificial system, but this can scarcely be maintained in the face of the first line of verse 8, where God is said definitely not to be reproving Israel for their *zebach*-offerings. There are indeed psalmists who deprecate the whole system of offerings of both types (Psalm 51.16), though even there a later editor seems to have made an addition to this Davidic psalm which contradicts the sentiment of the original author (verses 18 and 19). But this psalmist (50) was definitely in favour of *zebachs* (verse 8a) and also of *todahs* (thank-offerings, verse 14).

But what was actually the significance of the *zebach*? Writers on the origin of sacrifice have tended to assume that all sacrifices of whatever type have one basic origin, gift to the god, or means of communication with him, or means of liberating life, and so forth. It is more likely that different types of sacrifices had different origins, and possible too, as MM. Hubert and Mauss suggested in 1899, that no single idea underlies any one type. It is probable that the idea behind the *'olah* (whole burnt offering) was that of a gift to the god, to acknowledge his lordship and his ownership, to placate him, to feed him, or any one or more of the four objects mentioned. On the other hand, the idea behind the *zebach* necessarily is bound up with the fact that it was the worshippers who ate most of it. The word originally referred to any kind of slaughter for food, and even in the time of the two monarchies this was the dominant idea. In the country, the beast was slaughtered on a stone. This stone was called the *mizbeach*, the place of slaughter, and this was the word which later meant 'altar'. One particular portion was assigned to the god, the blood was all poured out over the stone, and the rest provided the common meal. When the worship was centralized at Jerusalem, regulations had to be made for the slaughter of beasts for food (Lev. 17.13-14), because no man could go all the way to Jerusalem every time he wanted mutton or beef for dinner. He could have gone easily to the local shrine, and probably the original custom of slaughtering beasts did develop into this, but Jerusalem was altogether too far away for most. The important thing about this regulation is that it makes it quite clear that the essential point about the *zebach* was that it was something which ordinary people ate.

In the case of the animal which was brought to the temple for the sacred meal, i.e. the true sacrificial *zebach*, the priest laid his hands upon it and consecrated it. The animal thus became ' holy '. When the animal was slaughtered, the blood was poured out at the foot of the altar, since blood was always regarded as being *tabu* for man, but the remainder of the food was eaten by the worshippers, apart from the portion which was allocated to God by way of tribute, since none may come before Him without a gift. It was in this way that the worshipper was able to partake of ' life ', that mysterious non- or half-material essence of which, according to the most primitive notions, both gods and men needed to partake. Advancing ideas of a personal ' Other ' (developing from an original Otherness) transformed this sacred meal into ' eating the god ' and so partaking of the divine nature. This, as we understand Psalm 50, is the type of sacrifice which the psalmist emphasizes at the expense of the other. He desires that men should eat of that holiness which is the inner life of the true Israel. Something of this is in the minds of many Christians at the Lord's Supper, Holy Communion, Eucharist, Mass. They believe that they ' eat God ', though they explain the mode of it in different ways, some of them quite abhorrent to other Christians. I judge that Romanists seek to explain the way in which this is done by their doctrine of Transubstantiation, Lutherans by Consubstantiation, and so forth. For my part, I would say that the elements (the bread and the wine) are symbols, but that we do eat His body and drink His blood by faith in the heart. On these general grounds, I judge this particular psalmist to be in very truth one of those who blazed the trail for better things. He was against gifts to God, knowing that the one gift which God requires is the thankful heart. He was wholly in favour of that type of sacrifice which involved the worshipper partaking of the divine nature, 'eating the God', building up his spiritual body with heavenly Food.

What God desires most of all is set forth in verses 14 and 15.

> Sacrifice to–God a–thank-offering:
> And–fulfil to–the–Most–High thy–vows;
> And–call–to–me in–the–day–of distress:
> I–will–rescue–thee, and–thou–shalt–honour–me.

The Hebrew word *todah* can mean either a certain type of flesh offering (Lev. 7.12, P) or a thanksgiving song (six times in the Psalter definitely of a song, and thrice also in this sense outside the Psalter; but twice inside the Psalter of a flesh offering, 107.22 and 116.17, and possibly twice more, here and 56.12). But the use of the verb 'slaughter' (translated 'sacrifice') turns the scale here in favour of the opinion that the psalmist means an actual flesh offering (verses 14 and 22). The *todah* (thank-offering) is a particular type of *zebach* (Lev. 7.11, where the Hebrew says *shelamim*, which is short for *zebach-shelamim*, usually translated 'peace-offering', but better 'health-offering', and so also is the *neder* (vow, cf. latter half of verse 14). Evidently, then, when the psalmist refers to the two main types of sacrifices in verse 8 (*zebach*, the shared meal, and *'olah*, wholly burned on the altar), he is all in favour of the former because he is thinking of two special such sacrifices, the thank-offering and the vow. These are definitely offerings which are linked up with days of distress, calling upon God and finding deliverance.

Here it is that the psalmist gets right down to the root of the matter. He knew that the God of Israel is essentially the Saviour-God who rescues Israel. When men worship God, they must worship Him because they know that He has always rescued them in the day of their distress. As verse 23 says:

> He–that–sacrifices a–thank-offering honours–me,
> And–he–that–sets (his) way
> I–will–show–him the–salvation–of God.

Some scholars would read 'and he that fulfils his vow' instead of 'he that sets (his) way'. The changes which such an alteration involves are not large, and the proposed reading certainly fits in well with the second section of the psalm. But the third section (verses 16-21) seem to demand something to do with a man ordering his way aright. Whilst the present reading is unsatisfactory, something of the same sentiment seems to be required. The psalmist knows that God has no need to eat meat or drink blood. There is nothing at all that He needs in order to keep Him alive, and still less can man give Him anything. But that which God does earnestly desire is that in every time of trouble men should turn to Him. Then once again He can exercise His sovereign right as Saviour, and bring deliverance. And in so far as God has any pleasure in the sacrificial system, it is in those gift offerings and ceremonies which are the outcome of gratefulness and thankfulness because of mercies received from God.

The third section of the psalm (verses 16-21) is God's declaration to the wicked. Here the wicked man is not the man who openly flaunts every vestige of religion and outwardly scorns such things. Nor is he the man who simply ignores religion and, in modern terms, 'does not go in for that sort of thing'. The wicked man of whom the psalmist speaks is the man who says one thing with his lips and another thing with his life. He is the man who speaks the words of religion and maintains the outward forms of religion, but at the same time makes terms with evil. The psalmist does not charge his wicked man with theft or with adultery, but he does charge him with consorting with thieves and adulterers. For the rest, the wicked man sins with his tongue. He 'pairs up' with deceit, and when he sits and talks with his own blood-brother, he is always finding fault and blame and blemish.

The psalmist is thus not speaking against 'vile and filthy sinners', but rather against 'those who have long distinguished themselves from the herd of vicious wretches' (the phrases are taken from John Wesley's *Journal* for May 14, 1738), and pride themselves on being broad-minded. All this is a strong criticism of those who are satisfied with the outward forms of religion, and/or who think that the precise repetition of prescribed forms is enough. Here again there is a dangerous course with a Scylla on one side and a Charybdis on the other. Where there is ritual practice, it is easy for the primitive notion of early man to survive and for us to imagine that the actual performance of the rite is in itself effective. This can lead, though by no means necessarily, to a division between ritual observance and the practice of daily living, and thus to the thoroughly anomalous position which the psalmist is criticizing. On the other hand, to discard all ritualistic practice on the ground of its danger of abuse, can lead, though once again by no means necessarily, to a general looseness and vagueness in religious ideas and in prayer which is destructive, rather than constructive, of sound religion. In each case, the psalmist provides the solution. The secret is a true thankfulness to God, and an ever-present consciousness of His redeeming grace. Given this true thankfulness of heart, both ways are paths to God. Without it, both ways lead to disaster.

# VI

## *Psalm 73*

# THE PROSPERITY OF THE WICKED

THE PSALMIST is in serious difficulties concerning the problem of the fate of the good man. He believes that in this world the good man should prosper and live long. Equally, he believes that the wicked man should meet with an early death after a life of poverty and trouble. He sets out with this firm conviction of his in the first couplet:

> Nay:
> Good to–the–upright (is) El,
> God (is good) to–the–pure–of heart.  (v. 1).

The usual translation of the opening word is 'surely', but this is an error. The word always has in it an element of contradiction. It is used when the writer is setting out deliberately to deny some proposition, whether explicitly or implicitly expressed. Here he means, 'Nay, in spite of all that people say, and in spite of all that I have seen, I still do earnestly maintain that God is good to the upright man.' A similar error is usually made in the translation of Psalm 23. The true interpretation is, 'Nay: Jehovah is my Shepherd . . . and this I maintain in spite of everything. In spite of deep and dark ravines, in spite of enemies ringing round, I am still nevertheless sure that God's goodness and mercy (*chesed*) will follow me as long as I live.' In both psalms the same Hebrew word *ṭob* (good, goodness) is

used. It means general well-being, with everything going
well. This is the meaning of the same word in the first
chapter of Genesis, when it is said that 'God saw that it
was good'. God is not passing a moral judgment on His
work in Creation up to that stage. There is no suggestion
in chapter 1 of a pristine moral goodness in Creation, for
Genesis 1 has no point of contact with the next three chapters except that it happens to come next before them in the
actual text. The phrase means that God looked at what
He had so far done, and He pronounced it to be satisfactory. At this stage and at that stage, His review of
what He had already done was that so far all was working
well.

An emendation has been assumed in the first line of the
couplet, and it affects the second part of the verse in the
usual English translation. The Hebrew text reads 'to
Israel', but it is generally agreed by the scholars that it is
better to divide the word into two, and to read 'to the upright' and 'El'. This enables the word '*Elohim* (God)' to
be transferred to the second line of the couplet. It helps
both rhythm and sense, because now we have a true and
elegant couplet after the best Hebrew style, and further,
the verse agrees with the rest of the psalm. The psalmist is
not discussing God's goodness to Israel, but he is discussing
God's attitude to the upright man within Israel.

Having declared in the first verse his theme and his un-
alterable conviction, the psalmist goes on to speak of his
sore distress:

As–for–me, almost my–feet had–faltered,
My–steps had–well–nigh been–halted. (v. 2).

He had very nearly lost his faith. His almost granite
conviction had been shaken. He was jealous of the wicked
man, for he saw how healthy and vigorous he was. (The
Hebrew word *shalom*, usually translated 'peace', often
means 'good health'; cf. Isaiah 53.5, 'The chastening

which brought us health, fell upon him; and through his stripes, there was healing to us.') The wicked have no griping pangs. Their bellies are plump and well-rounded. (The Hebrew text has 'in their death', but once again it is better to split the consonants differently, and to read 'to them' in the first half of the line, and 'perfect' or 'well-rounded' with the second line of the couplet.) They do not share frail man's trouble, nor are they smitten with disease like ordinary human kind. And so they swagger around in their arrogance as though they are making a necklace of it, and they are shamelessly rapacious, flauntingly rapacious as if they are wearing a gaudy cloak. Their iniquity (so the Greek Version) issues forth from their midriff fat; their pet plans tumble over one another. They mock, they talk wickedly and overbearingly from their exalted station. They set their mouth in the heavens, and their tongue stalks through the earth. (Verse 10 is unintelligible, and any emendations are mostly guesswork.) They say 'How does God know?' and 'Is there knowledge in the Most High?' This, says the psalmist, is what the wicked are like. They are always at ease, as they heap up their wealth.

From this picture of the lawless and ostentatious affluence of the wicked, the psalmist turns to his own situation. He says (verse 13) that he has cleansed his own heart, that he has washed his hands in true repentance, but that it has all been in vain. He still is being afflicted day by day, and every morning his troubles are there to reprove him. He is tempted to tell aloud the story of his woes and doubts, but he refrains lest he should make faith more difficult for God's children. The fact that he has doubts and uncertainties is no reason why he should parade them in order to make other folks doubtful and uncertain also. He tries very hard to understand it all, because it is a serious trouble to him. At last he enters God's sanctuary, and then and there it is that he comes to understand what is the fate of the wicked.

The solution with which the psalmist finds himself content is to be found in verse 18. Nay (once more the same particle as that with which the psalm opens), they may be flourishing now, but as a matter of fact God has placed them on very slippery places (the Hebrew word is in the plural to denote intensity). He is sure to bring them down suddenly in respect of their great illusions.

The Hebrew here has the plural once more, to denote intensity. The commentators usually say that the Hebrew is here at fault, and they commonly alter the vowels so as to read 'to great destruction'. This is what both the Authorized and the Revised Versions have done. Perhaps this is the right thing to do, but 'great illusions' is nevertheless a good parallel to the 'very slippery places' of the first line of the couplet.

With reference to the translation 'bring them down suddenly', the Hebrew verb *naphal* does not always mean 'fall'. It sometimes means 'swoop down suddenly', the emphasis being on the speed of the descent. Cf. Amos 3.5: 'Does a bird swoop down suddenly to the ground, where there is no decoy?' Also, cf. Genesis 24.64, of Rebekah alighting hurriedly from her camel when she sees Isaac; and again II Kings 5.21 of Naaman's hurried descent from his chariot when he sees Gehazi running after him.

Further, the verb is in the perfect tense, and is unfortunately so translated in the English Versions. This applies also to the next verse. Actually they have not slipped up and fallen down suddenly. They are strutting along in full pride. The use of the perfect tense is here idiomatic, and is either that use known to the grammarians as 'the perfect of certainty' or else it is a use of the perfect describing an action which is so nearly come to pass that it can practically be regarded as having already taken place. The perfect thus expressed the psalmist's conviction that the fate of the wicked is nevertheless satisfactorily disastrous in spite of the present appearances.

The psalmist continues (verse 19): How certain it is that

they will come to destruction suddenly. They will assuredly come to an end, be utterly finished off because of dire calamity. (Once more we have a plural word in the Hebrew to indicate the fulness and the completeness of the disaster. The word actually used is the 'nightmare' word of Job 27.20.) They will cease to exist (reading *'enam* for *'adonai* in verse 20a) just as a dream vanished upon waking. When Thou (the psalmist speaks to God) rousest up, Thou wilt regard them as a worthless phantom.

The conclusion of the psalm begins with verse 21. The psalmist confesses that his heart (i.e. his inmost being) was embittered, and that he was pierced through and through with envy. He admits that he was brutishly dull and did not understand. 'I was very beast' (this is S. R. Driver's happy translation of the plural, another instance of this psalmist's frequent use of this idiom) 'in my thought of Thee.' But now, says the psalmist, I am conscious of being always in Thy presence. Thou hast grasped me by my right hand. Thou wilt guide me with Thy counsel, and in the end Thou wilt bring me to prosperity. Whom have I but Thee, either in the heavens above or on the earth beneath? And being with Thee, I desire none other, either in the heavens or on the earth. (The 'heavens' and the 'earth' have been repeated here in order to make it quite clear that the psalmist is talking topographically of the sky above and the ground underneath. He is not saying any-thing at all in this couplet about Heaven as a place-state after death.) My flesh and my heart may fail, but God is my portion for ever. (The phrase 'O Rock of my heart' has been inserted after 'fail', perhaps by the psalmist him-self, perhaps by a copyist.)

This much, then, says the psalmist, is certain. Those who are far away from God are certain to perish. God will certainly destroy every man who seeks intercourse with other deities instead of with Him. As for me, concludes the psalmist, being close to God is my best policy. I have fixed my refuge in Him. The closing phrase 'to recount all thy works' is probably a later addition in the Hebrew. The Greek has added yet another phrase 'in the gates of Zion'.

The attitude of this psalmist with his theory of retribution, involving rewards and punishments for good and bad in this world, is usually called Deuteronomic. This is because, in the Old Testament, the full and formal expression of this doctrine is set forth in the Book of Deuteronomy. God there sets before the people the choice of a blessing and a curse (Deut. 30.19). The blessing will come to them if they hear and obey. (The Hebrew *shama*, usually translated 'hear, hearken', very often means 'hear and obey'.) But if they do not hear and obey, then the curse will come to them (Deut. 11.26-28). Retribution is direct and in this world. Further, the blessing will be realized in great prosperity, a numerous progeny and a long life. The curse is precisely the opposite of all this. An excellent picture of what Deuteronomic theory envisaged as the state of the truly pious and perfect man is to be seen in the first chapter of the Book of Job. The author of this prologue has done everything he can to build up his story. He begins with a picture of the upright man who is perfect in every possible respect. Job has seven sons, three daughters, large herds of every kind of domestic animal, and a tremendous household. He was the greatest and the most splendid of all the ancient desert chiefs, with his family feasting every evening, and crowds of retainers to fulfil his slightest desire. The picture is followed by one of a man upon whom the whole of the Deuteronomic curse has fallen, with the sole exception of sudden death. The man's sons are all dead. His whole property has gone. He is an outcast, smitten with the most loathsome of diseases, one which was regarded as cutting him off from both man and God. His very name has become a byword.

But this belief in rewards and punishments for good conduct and for bad conduct, all of them to be realized in this world, is not confined to the Book of Deuteronomy, nor is it Old Testament religion only. It is the common belief of men and women the whole world over, and nowhere is it more prevalent than in our own country. We all hear regularly, and sometimes we ourselves ask, 'What have I done to deserve this?' and 'Why should this happen to me?' The fact is that we all believe with varying degrees of conviction that good conduct should be followed in this world with happiness and prosperity. Added to this is a decidedly rosy view of our own attainments in good works, with the result that we feel ourselves hardly done by when things go wrong.

In the Old Testament this problem of the prosperity of the wicked was created by the growth of the understanding of the nature of God. So long as God was thought of as being capricious and non-moral, there was no problem. He is just as likely to prosper the wicked and the good. In fact, since He Himself is regarded as capricious and caring only for getting His own way, the presumption is that the same sort of thing is to be expected here. This kind of God has no standards of rightness or morality. Presumably He is pleased with presents, and the more costly the presents, the more likely He is to be pleased. Those who can give Him the most expensive presents are the rich, so here is another reason why the rich may be expected to prosper. If, therefore, a righteous man prospers, it is not because of his righteousness, but because he has got on the right side of God. Equally, if the wicked man prospers, it is because he also has done the things that please God. Good conduct or bad conduct have neither of them anything to do with it. There is no condition of right or of wrong whereby the goodwill of such a god can be secured. Gifts and gifts alone are required. Perhaps this is why the 50th psalmist is against such ideas. There are innumerable traces of this belief in the Old Testament background, especially in the prophets, for this belief is one of the things against which the prophets ceaselessly thundered. The notable examples are Hosea 6.6 (For I desired *chesed*—faithfulness to the covenant—rather than *zebachs* and the knowledge of God rather than whole offerings); Micah 6.6-8 (with its conclusion, 'What doth the Lord demand of thee, but to do what is right, and to love *chesed* and to walk humbly with thy God? '); and Isaiah 1.10-17, with its violent tirade against men who trample the Temple courts, multiply every kind of religious rite, and neglect those social virtues and that moral behaviour which are essentially well-pleasing to the God of Israel. As Psalm 50.21 puts it, the mass of the people thought that God was altogether just like themselves, and that just as they were pleased with presents and gifts and bribes, so God also delighted in such things. But the prophets demanded right action; they knew that men must 'learn to do well; seek after justice; relieve the oppressed, take up the cause of the fatherless and the widow'. The prophets were saying this four hundred years before the time of Aristotle; they were saying this about the time when Rome was founded. Indeed, it is now being maintained more and more that sound ethical conduct was part of the Mosaic legislation, and that the teaching of these eighth century B.C. prophets was in part a revival of the teaching of Moses. This makes the beginnings of Hebrew ethical teaching earlier than the fall of Homer's Troy. Further, as we have already said, apart from the fact that the Greek ethical teaching was centuries later than that of the Hebrews, it developed differently. The Greek ethical thinkers developed their ideas of right conduct from human ideals, and then they realized that the gods must be at least as good as men. The gods could not be as capricious and as lustful as the Homeric gods. The Hebrew prophets began at the other end. It was from their insight into the nature of God that they formed their ideas of what was right for men. Men must be moral in deed and in thought, not because of any 'good for man', nor even because such conduct was good and desirable in itself. For the Hebrew prophets, men must be moral because it is the will of God that they shall be so. It was, as Micah 6.8 expresses it, a requirement laid down by God Himself, and He required such conduct because that is His nature.

But whatever belonged to the Mosaic code so far as sound ethical conduct was concerned, the prophets saw farther still into the nature of God. They realized that God had a particular care for the helpless ones in the land. As we have pointed out elsewhere, the reason for this emphasis historically may well have been that if righteousness is to be established in the land, the place where changes most need to be made is in connection with the circumstances of the poor and the helpless. In any case it came about that the righteousness of which the prophets spoke had, from the beginning, a more than ethical content. This is why the nursery of true religion was not in one of the conquering nations of the world, but in one of the conquered. It was not amongst the strong, but amongst the weak. And even in this small nation, the righteousness of which the prophets spoke was concerned with the unprivileged in Israel. The result of this is that, certainly from the eighth century onwards, the word *tsedaqah*, together with its masculine form *tsedeq* (the words usually translated 'righteousness') has tended to belong to the category of salvation at least as much as to the category of ethics. Indeed, there came a time in the early Christian era when the word *tsedaqah* could be contrasted with *din* (strict justice). The passage is to be found in the *Tosephta Sanhedrin* i, 3: 'Wherever there is *din*, there is no *tsedaqah*, and wherever there is *tsedaqah*, there is no *din*.' There is a story told of a judge who rightly convicted a defendant and fined him a sum of money. This, said the Rabbis, was *din* (strict justice). The judge then paid the fine himself. This, said the Rabbis, was *tsedaqah*.

It will be seen from this development, due in its beginning to the eighth century B.C. prophets, that the problem of the psalmist was greater even than could be involved in a simple, straightforward demand for individual justice. The problem of the unfortunate righteous man was serious enough according to the demands of strict justice. But *tsedaqah* tended always to mean more than strict justice. The problem was thus more serious, because they knew that God had a particular concern for the unprivileged and the down-trodden. The question was not only 'Why does not God see to it that there is individual justice in the world?' The question really was, 'If God has a particular care for the fatherless, the widow, the resident alien, in fact for everybody who is oppressed, then why does He allow me (the psalmist) to continue in distress and poverty in spite of sincere repentance?'

The psalmist's solution to his problem was a still firmer belief in orthodox doctrine. It is all true. God will certainly see to it that the righteous prosper, and that the wicked come to destruction. The wicked may be marching along at the present moment in arrogance and pride, but actually he is walking along a very treacherous and slippery road. Soon, perhaps very soon, perhaps at this very moment, he will meet with dreadful and irreparable disaster. It will be like waking from a dream. The dream suddenly goes. And so, in a moment, the whole prosperity of the wicked man will vanish. The psalmist tells himself he was foolish ever to doubt. He himself is continually in God's presence. It is merely a matter of time before this inner consciousness will blossom into outward fruit for all the world to see. The psalmist is perfectly satisfied. God is his, and he is God's. What more can any man desire? And the psalmist concludes with a final assurance that he need not worry about the fate of the wicked. God will see to that all right.

I have discussed elsewhere[1] the various reactions of the psalmist generally to this problem of suffering. One psalmist, an aged man, the author of Psalm 37, roundly declares that in all his long life he has never seen the righteous forsaken, nor his seed begging their bread. This psalmist is like the dormouse in Mr. A. A. Milne's *When we were very young*. The dormouse lived in a bed of delphiniums (blue) and geraniums (red). The doctor insisted on a bed

---

[1] *Have Faith in God*, 1935, pp. 57-104.

of chrysanthemums (yellow and white). But this prospect
made the poor little dormouse feel worse and worse, until
he hit on the idea of putting his paws to his eyes and lying
fast asleep on his front. And

> The dormouse lay happy, his eyes were so tight
> He could see no chrysanthemums, yellow or white,
> And all that he felt at the back of his head
> Were delphiniums (blue) and geraniums (red).

That was how the dormouse got well again. He closed his
eyes to what he could see, and held firmly to what he had
at the back of his head. The psalmist similarly closed his
eyes to all that he could see of the distress of the righteous
and of the prosperity of the wicked, and there right at the
back of his head, he held firmly to his doctrine of present
rewards and punishments. The seventy-first psalmist,
another old man, is still sure of the orthodox belief which
he has held all his life long, but his psalm is not so much a
determined steadfastness in the face of the facts as a path-
etic plea that God will not desert him in his old age. Both
aged men have this much in common, that they remain
steadfast and firm in their convictions. And so always with
all the psalmists. They bring forth all sorts of suggestions
and arguments to explain why the Deuteronomic scheme is
not working, but they never doubt the soundness of it.

The seventy-third psalmist was right in the main, though
not precisely as he himself stated it. The secret is to be
found in verse 23, where he says that he is continually with
God. The history of the exegesis of this and the succeeding
verse provides the true solution. It is indeed true that the
man who is 'continually with God' is the man who knows
that sense of ease and freedom from fear and anxiety which
we all earnestly desire. The problem is as to where and
how this security is to be found.

The Hebrew text admits of no doubt here as to what the
psalmist himself meant. He meant that God would keep a

firm hold of him here on earth and would ultimately bring him to the prosperity which he was sure his righteousness deserved. He meant prosperity here on earth, this side of the grave. He himself had no thought of any life beyond the grave. It is a false exegesis which sees here any reference to ideas of life after death. Verse 25 refers quite clearly to the heavens which are above us, and equally to the earth upon which we now live. It is nevertheless true that this verse was interpreted for many centuries to refer to the blessedness of a Heaven beyond the grave. Actually it was the demand for justice for the individual which led the Hebrews at long last to a belief in something more than the shadow-life of Sheol after death. It is quite wrong to assume that Hebrew ideas of life beyond the grave developed from their earlier ideas of Sheol, the lifeless abode of the dead. The belief arose from the conviction that somewhere, sometime, the righteous must ' see good '. This can be seen in the description of Sheol which is given in the Book of Enoch in chapter 22, a passage which is generally agreed to belong to the section dated *c*. 170 B.C. There are three hollow places, completely separated each from the other. In these three hollow places the spirits of the souls of the dead were believed to assemble till the great judgment. The first of these hollow places was for the righteous, and they were kept safe there until the judgment day when they were raised up to enter the Messianic Kingdom. The second of the hollow places is for those sinners who have not been punished on earth for sins committed during their lifetime. Here they suffered great pain and torment until the judgment day, when they were to be bound for ever and ever. The third of the hollow places was for those sinners who had been punished on earth for their sins. ' They shall not be slain in the day of judgment, neither shall they be raised from thence.' It will be seen that the criterion throughout is strict justice. The fundamental idea is that the Deuteronomic principle is sound, if not in this world, then in the next. It is the righteous alone who find a place in the

Messianic Kingdom. The wicked must be punished. If they have been punished on earth for their sins, then that is that, and that is the end of them. If they have not been punished on earth for their sins, then they must be punished hereafter, and when the punishment is complete, that is an end of them. In the parable of Dives and Lazarus (Luke 16.19-31), Lazarus is represented as being in the first of the hollow places, there waiting for the judgment day, when he will be raised to the Messianic Kingdom. Dives is in the second of the hollow places, where he is paying the price for his sins for which he never suffered upon earth.

This belief in justice for the individual has had a great deal to do also with the Christian development of ideas of the after life, particularly in respect of ideas of heaven. We need go no farther back in this country than a century ago, when the hymns of the common people were full of hope of rest and peace beyond the River. They sang:

> On Jordan's stormy banks I stand,
> And cast a wistful eye
> To Canaan's fair and happy land,
> Where my possessions lie.

The last line of this not-very-good verse (from the literary point of view) explains why there was so much of this hope of heaven in their hymns. It was because they had no possessions here, and they knew right well that if ever they were going to have any possessions worth talking about, it would have to be 'beyond the River'. This same situation explains why it is that Negro Spirituals have almost exclusively this same motif. They looked forward to the time, for instance, when they were 'going to walk all over God's heaven'. This was because on earth they had no right to walk anywhere, and did not even possess their own bodies. Heaven, for negro slaves and for British unprivileged, was 'beyond the River'. That was where their hopes and longings were to be satisfied. It ill becomes a comfortable generation to jeer at hymns which speak of this world as 'a vale of tears'.

But in these latter years, even the common people have found a share in the prosperity of the country, beginning, for the most part, from the passing of the Old Age Pensions Act. The result of this is to be seen partly in the hymns which have been written and sung during the last fifty years or so. There is far less in them of a heaven beyond the River, and far more of a heaven to be realized this side. And further, those who have been brought up to think of heaven in terms of personal enjoyment and rewards, have naturally tended to by-pass religion altogether. Why worry over much about a religion which promises happiness beyond when a man can get all the happiness he can enjoy this side of the grave? To this extent religious people are as much responsible as anybody else for the decline of religion in modern times. Preachers of the past generation, and some of this generation, have contributed to this situation. We have talked not so much about heaven in an after-life, as about the Kingdom of God which is to be set up on earth. It is to be realized in better social conditions and in a growing share for the workers of the profits of industry. It is to be realized in a world of equal opportunity, where all men can obtain leisure, amusement, and good things of this life generally. All the time, the dominant motif has been that of justice for the individual and fair dealing all round. And equally the tendency has been to interpret these delights in terms of material possessions or of aesthetic delights. The Hebrews of old time and the Jews of later times have not been by any means alone in thinking in terms of physical and material well-being in association with the individual and his demands for personal justice.

The true solution is that heaven is not to be found only beyond the River of Death, nor is it to be found only this side of that river. The solution is to be found in the full Christian development of the first half of verse 24: 'Nevertheless I am continually with thee.' The reward of the

Christian is that happiness and serenity of spirit which is to be found in true fellowship, with God—'continually with thee'. This peace and serenity is the gift of God. It is 'by grace through faith', where grace is the free gift of God, and faith means complete trust in God and full reliance upon Him by man. Here we are in the realm of personal religion, a man's own experience of the presence of God.

There are many men and women who claim to be Christian and think of Christianity in the main as a set of moral principles. That is what those people must mean who say that Britain is a Christian country. They are decidedly optimistic, even then, but if they are not thinking in terms of moral human conduct, then their words have no meaning at all. Such conduct involves justice between man and man, and, theoretically at least, between class and class, and colour and colour. It involves a certain amount of generosity in thought and action, which goes, in selected circumstances, beyond the range of what is strictly just. But, generally, it is personal justice which comes first, and the generosity comes out of the overplus. These are the standards of ordinary, decent people. It is agreed that if all men lived up to these standards, this country and indeed the whole world, would be a vastly better place than it is. But all this is not the essence of Christianity, because Christianity is first and foremost a relationship with God. It is a personal relationship, and from the human side it is a matter of love and trust, complete love and utter trust. It is out of this personal relationship with God that there emerges the true serenity of the Christian life. So far as a man's relationship with others is concerned, it involves the exercise of Christian love, that same utterly and absolutely unselfish love which was manifested in the Lord Jesus Christ. This is why those reform movements which have made this country a much better place for the poor and the unprivileged have had their origin almost entirely in the work of individual Christians, who have done what they have done because they were Christians. Those who say that 'religion is dope for the masses', and deny that Christianity has ever done anything for ordinary people, are saying what is not true. It is true that the churches as organized bodies have tended to be against change, and generally conservative enough to give some substance to Paul Radin's jibe that the history of religion has been the story of an unholy alliance between the king and the priest. This is because the pace of any organization of whatever kind tends to be the pace of the slowest members. At the same time it is true that the reform movements of the past have been definitely Christian in origin. They sprang largely, as a matter of fact, out of the general impetus upon all classes of the Methodist revival of the eighteenth century. Christian men and women were responsible for the initiation of reform in prisons, work-houses, amongst orphans and strays, trade unions, schools for the children of ordinary people. And Christians, when they have been truly Christian, have always known that they must be in the van in every movement which has as its object the betterment of human kind.

But, however much the Christian may have been anxious to make this world a better place for all men and women, he has always known that his true happiness is not to be found outside, but inside, in that confidence and serenity which comes from being 'continually with God'. The great weakness of so much that has passed for Christianity is that so often our love for God has been at root selfish. It is a travesty of Christian love when we love God in order that we may be happy, or because of something that may happen to us because of it. True Christian love is wholly unselfish, and the Christian loves God because God has first loved him, out of a sense of complete gratefulness that God has done for him what he could never have done for himself. We need to realize that there are three distinct types of love, different types which we confuse at our peril. First, there is that self-love which is embedded deep in human nature, a corrupting selfishness which time and again has ruined all man's efforts, so that those things of the natural world which most should help him towards betterment have ended in causing destruction and death. This self-love is part of human nature. It is natural for us to be like this, natural to look out for ourselves, natural to resent being put down, natural to resent being placed in an inferior position, and so getting no more than a small part of our share when there are others who obviously get a great deal more than their share. This self-love has played a dominant part in the development of the world, and it is at the heart of evolutionary doctrine. It shows itself as the motif of selection and the impulse to survival, an impulse which becomes growingly self-conscious the 'higher' we climb in the scale. This same struggle for survival and urge for wider spheres of influence has become in our day a menace to the whole human race. What then is its solution?

One solution that is offered is to establish amongst men give-and-take, a true brotherly love. This is the type of love which the Greeks called *philia*. There is no doubt that if this sentiment could be universally established, all would be well. But this involves a radical change in that self-love (*eros*) which is at the heart of human nature. Many moderns maintain that this *eros* can be sublimated into *philia* by a sound and carefully-planned education. Perhaps this is so, but if it is so, it is not to be accomplished by an education which itself is based upon *eros*, and that is the case with much that passes for education to-day. It is based on the rights of the individual, on the right to self-expression, and the necessity of not violating human rights generally. This emphasis is but natural in non-totalitarian countries, especially since we have seen so much sorrow and tribulation from the annihilation of individual rights by the totalitarian state. The peril of this continued emphasis on the rights of the individual, where even the smallest child has its own rights, is that it tends to install more firmly than ever that self-love which is the root of our modern troubles.

The Christian solution is that there is a third type of

love, Christian love, *agape*. This word *agape* is a Christian word. It is the word used in the New Testament in the first place for God's love for man, and in the second place for the Christian's love for his fellows. This is the word used in I Corinthians 13, translated 'charity' in the Authorized Version, and 'love' in the Revised Version. A close examination of I Corinthians 13 will show how different in essence this *agape* is from *philia*. After all, it was not *philia* (brotherly love, give-and-take) which brought the Lord Jesus Christ into this world to die on the Cross. It was *agape,* the utterly selfless love of God, who loves not only those who are worth loving, but also those who are not worth loving. Here was no slightest semblance of *eros*, and no slightest thought of self. The true happiness of the Christian is to be found in the world of *agape,* that immortal love of God, because of which He 'was in Christ reconciling the world unto himself'. This 'heaven' is neither this side of the grave only, nor the other side of the grave only. It is independent of things, and independent of everything and everybody except only God Himself. The psalmist was right, but we need the full revelation of God in Christ to know it.

# INDEX

## SUBJECTS

121

# BIBLICAL REFERENCES

*(The figures printed in italics refer to
page numbers in the book)*